❧ Almost ❧
PERFECT CRIMES

Mini-Mysteries for You to Solve

Hy Conrad

Illustrated by Lucy Corvino

Sterling Publishing Co., Inc. New York

To J. J.,
there are not words enough

Edited by Jeanette Green

Library of Congress Cataloging-in-Publication Data

Conrad, Hy.
  Almost perfect crimes : mini-mysteries for you to solve / by Hy
Conrad ; illustrated by Lucy Corvino.
    p.   cm.
  Includes index.
  ISBN 0-8069-3807-2
  1. Puzzles.   2. Detective and mystery stories.   3. Literary
recreations.   I. Corvino, Lucy, ill.   II. Title.
GV1507.D4C66   1995
793.73—dc20   95-20065

7   9   10   8   6

Published by Sterling Publishing Company, Inc.
387 Park Avenue South, New York, N.Y. 10016
© 1995 by Hy Conrad
Distributed in Canada by Sterling Publishing
% Canadian Manda Group, One Atlantic Avenue, Suite 105
Toronto, Ontario, Canada M6K 3E7
Distributed in Great Britain and Europe by Cassell PLC
Wellington House, 125 Strand, London WC2R 0BB, England
Distributed in Australia by Capricorn Link (Australia) Pty Ltd.
P.O. Box 6651, Baulkham Hills, Business Centre, NSW 2153, Australia
Manufactured in the United States of America

Sterling ISBN 0-8069-3807-2

Contents

Introduction to Murder

These puzzles are not easy. I'm not trying to discourage you, especially if you haven't yet bought the book; I'm just trying to prepare you. Take your time with these mysteries. Relax. Read them more than once, thinking through each clue. Not only will this give you a better chance to solve the cases, but it will increase your enjoyment. It took me a long time to come up with these murder mysteries, to figure out the most devilish yet honest ways of deceiving the reader. Like many mystery lovers, I have always lived for the *Aha!*, that magic moment when everything makes sense. If you become too impatient with a mystery, you'll miss the Aha's.

A word about format. It's really self-explanatory. First you read a story, then you look up in the Evidence section of the book the piece(s) of evidence you'd like to see from the list following the story. In the Evidence section, in alphabetical order, you'll find these eight files and reports: Affidavit File, Autopsy Reports, Crime Scene Reports, Lab & Hospital Reports, Miscellaneous Examinations, Miscellaneous Searches, Research, and Wills & Insurance. Locate the story title (also in alphabetical order) within the given file. After consulting these files, you may want to check the Analysis of Evidence section, and finally the Solutions section. Again, stories in these sections can be found in alphabetical order.

Try not to form a theory before examining the clues. And

don't worry if you need to look at all the clues from the Evidence section before light dawns. Most cases here can be solved with two or three clues, but I personally couldn't do it. Consider yourself a sleuth if you don't have to peek at the Solutions. But good sleuths should be able to use information from the Evidence section without having to refer to the Analysis of Evidence section.

What if a piece of evidence, such as a ballistics test, seems crucial but is not offered as a clue? What if it forms an essential part of proving your budding theory but isn't given? This means that (a) your theory is dead wrong and the ballistics test isn't pertinent, or (b) your theory is correct, but by providing a ballistics test report I would be shouting out the answer. Usually it's (a).

A final note: don't overload. No matter how much fun you're having, try to control yourself. Don't try to solve too many of these mysteries too close together. Even the most enjoyable and ingenious mysteries lose their ability to please when crowded together in your mind. Do one a day. That way, the book will seem longer.

Hy Conrad

Video Violence

The tabloid television show "Exposé" was in a ratings slump when its host, Renaldo Jones, decided to expose the Mob. The Mob didn't seem thrilled by the publicity. Threatening letters and phone calls followed each new broadcast, but "Exposé"'s viewership suddenly soared. Renaldo took the threats in stride, installing a security system in his country house and boldly continuing his series of fearless investigations.

The murders occurred one Saturday in late October. Four people were in residence at the country house—Renaldo; his wife, Jane; Fred Fleer, the show's producer; and Gregory, their head camera operator. It was a working weekend and Fred started the morning meeting by suggesting that the Mob was old news and that "Exposé" should move on to a new subject.

"No way," Renaldo barked. "Two more weeks and I'll have the New York families cracked wide open. I've got some new sources you wouldn't believe." He sprang to his feet. "C'mon, Greg. We've got promos to tape."

Renaldo disabled the alarm. He told his wife to reset it as soon as they left; then he took Gregory with his video gear and headed out the door. Within minutes they were surrounded by brilliant sugar maples. Tape was rolling. And that was when the assassin appeared from behind a rock.

The figure was dressed in camouflage fatigues, gloves, and a ski mask. Before either man could react, the assassin raised a handgun and shot. Renaldo screamed and grabbed his leg, just below the knee. A circle of blood oozed through the fabric as the television star collapsed. The figure didn't fire again but simply turned and vanished into the woods.

"I can't move," Renaldo moaned. "Get help. No, you're turned around. The house is that way. And don't get lost."

But Gregory did. He raced frantically, trying to keep a straight path and failing to recognize any landmarks. It was 10 minutes before he ran into another human being, a neighboring farmer. The two men called the police then ran back into the woods carrying a makeshift stretcher. When they found Renaldo, he had already bled to death from the wound.

The second corpse was waiting back at Renaldo's house.

Fred Fleer greeted the police in a state of shock. He had been upstairs, he said, on the phone to New York. Bits of noise drifted up the from the hall, but he ignored them. Then came the gunshot. Fred ran to the staircase. There at the bottom, by the open front door, stood a man in full camouflage. At the man's feet was Jane Jones, lying in a pool of blood. "The guy was just standing there," Fred stammered. "When he saw me, he brandished the weapon at me but didn't shoot. He just stood there for a second, then disappeared out the door."

Jane had been shot once in the chest at close range. The police wondered what made her open the door. She had taken the threats even more seriously than her husband. There was a peephole in the door and the alarm had been turned on. Why in the world would she turn off the system and open the door to a gunman wearing fatigues and a mask?

As the homicide team continued the investigation, other oddities popped up, making the case seem more than an assassination. The .38 used in both murders was discovered just a stone's throw from Renaldo's body. The fatigues, mask, and gloves were found in a potting shed not far from the house.

A confused sergeant tried to piece it together. "Renaldo was shot first. Then the killer goes to the house and shoots Jane. He hides his disguise, in the shed, then returns to Renaldo, wipes off the gun and drops it." The officer frowned. "Why didn't he keep the disguise on? And why would he dump the gun right there instead of disposing of it? It doesn't make sense."

Whodunit? (1) Who killed Renaldo? (2) Who killed Jane? (3) How were the murders committed?

Evidence *This crime can be solved in 3 clues.*
- Gregory's Video (Miscellaneous Examinations)
- Fred's Testimony (Affidavit File)
- Crime Scene Report (The Woods)
- Renaldo's Autopsy Report
- Master Bedroom (Miscellaneous Searches)

Checking Out

Scotty adjusted his black bow tie, then knocked. "Room service." After his third unanswered knock, Scotty used his pass key to open the hotel room door. "Mr. Williams?"

The waiter had just pushed the cart into the room when he saw the body. It was Mr. Williams, naked except for the blood. A ribbon of red snaked across the carpet, ending by the dresser. In front of the dresser lay the middle-aged guest, his head bashed in. Scotty ran out of the room and straight into a maid who was bringing fresh towels to the room next door.

The Chantel was one of Manhattan's poshest small hotels. But there had been a rash of burglaries here during the past few months. At first the police assumed this was the result of one, a burglary gone fatally wrong. They soon changed their minds. "Nothing was taken," a sergeant pointed out. "His wallet's in plain sight there on the table. And there's jewelry on the dresser, both his and his wife's."

The captain in charge was inspecting the carpet. "Williams must have lived for a few minutes after the attack. He was hit first over here. Bag that telephone, Hopper. Torn out of the wall. Could be our weapon." The captain waited until the sergeant had done so. "Several hard hits. He collapsed by the table. The killer walked out, left him for dead. Then, when he was alone, our Williams recovered enough to drag himself across the room. Not to the phone, which wasn't working, but . . . Hmm."

Kneeling down by the dresser, he pried open the corpse's two clenched fists. In the right was a wedding band, the victim's own wedding band. In the left was a tie tack. The captain stood up and glanced around. There was no pen or paper anywhere in sight.

"The man knows he's dying. So he takes off his wedding ring, keeps it in his fist. Then he drags himself across to the dresser, pulls himself up, and grabs a pearl tie tack."

"According to the hotel staff, Mr. Williams's wife is named Pearl." The sergeant looked up from his notes and smiled. "Bingo! Don't you see? The wedding ring? The pearl? He was trying to tell us his attacker's identity—his wife, Pearl."

The sergeant's theory was smashed two minutes later when Pearl herself walked in, having just returned from a Broadway matinee. They sat her down with a brandy and gently questioned her. "You may as well know," Pearl confessed between sobs. "Bob Williams wasn't my husband."

She downed the rest of the drink. "We're both sales reps. Different companies. We first met here in New York a year ago. Bob has a wife in Boston. I have a husband in Philadelphia. Once every few months we arrange to come here on business. We have two or three great days together, then go back to our lives. No one gets hurt. Not until now, I guess."

The police spent the next two days interviewing the principals and taking their statements. At the time of the murder, Pearl Lowe claimed to be at a performance of *Cats* and produced her theater ticket and program as evidence. No one could recall seeing her around the hotel during the time in question.

Dr. Lamar Lowe claimed to know nothing of his wife's infidelity. His alibi? He'd been alone in his Philadelphia office, on the phone, updating his billing system and sending faxes to a few colleagues in California.

Ms. Emma Williams worked as a flight attendant, based in Boston. On the day of her husband's death, she was on call, staying close to her phone in case she was needed for a flight.

"None of their alibis is perfect," the captain whined. "So, what we got here is a naked man clutching a ring and a tie tack. What the heck was going on?"

Whodunit?   (1) Who killed Bob Williams?   (2) Why?   (3) What was the meaning of the ring and pearl tie tack?

Evidence   *This crime can be solved in 3 clues.*
- Crime Scene Report
- Autopsy Report
- Search for Murder Weapon (Miscellaneous Searches)
- Hotel Closet (Miscellaneous Searches)
- Scotty's Testimony (Affidavit File)

The Bearded Lady

For years Ben and Vicky Livery forced themselves to be nice to Uncle Joshua, always assuming that he would die and leave them his fortune. When that happy day arrived and the old millionaire keeled over from a stroke, the Livery siblings were faced with a rude surprise.

"Your uncle changed his will," Joshua's lawyer informed them. "It seems that forty years ago, when Mr. Livery was a youth, he fell in love with a girl named Amelia Perdue. They were engaged to be married. But Amelia had a twin brother, Alex. Alex Perdue talked his sister out of the marriage. Soon afterwards, the Perdues moved to Australia."

"Don't tell me he put this woman in his will!" Ben pulled nervously on his goatee. "How much does she inherit?"

George Trent cleared his throat. "Toward the end of his life, it seems the old bachelor began to fondly recall his one great romance. Amelia gets everything, I'm afraid. If she's still alive, that is, and if I can find her."

For months brother and sister lived in hope. The first rumors to surface were that Amelia had become a nun and died in a Melbourne convent. This, of course, was too good to be true. Eventually the lawyer located the old heiress, flying her back to Boston to claim her windfall.

On the second evening of her American visit, Amelia was seated in the place of honor in the Livery dining room. She was a big-boned woman in her late sixties, dressed in a prudish concoction of satin. She tried smiling at Joshua's niece and nephew but was rewarded with only stony glares.

"You've checked her out?" Vicky asked the lawyer. "This is the real Amelia Perdue and not some impostor?"

Trent nodded. "Birth certificate. Bank cards. Her passport is ancient, but the photo leaves no doubt. Plus, she knows all the details of Joshua's life forty years ago. It's her."

"I know how hard it must be. A stranger from the past popping up like this." The elderly woman rose to her feet. "I won't be staying any longer than necessary." She gulped several times, her cameo choker bobbing up and down. Then she doubled over in pain and fainted dead away.

Dr. David Denton lived alone next door. He was called in to examine the unconscious woman in her bedroom. Before leaving, he spoke to George Trent. "Food poisoning," Denton whispered gravely. "She'll be all right, but . . . I would keep a very careful eye on her if I were you."

Amelia spent much of the next day recovering, while Trent kept a nervous watch on the Liverys, personally monitoring all the food going into the old woman's room. Around 10 that night, just as the cook was preparing to leave, a gunshot rang out. More surprising than the shot itself was the fact that the sound had come from next door.

When the sheriff's department broke into the Denton house, they found Dr. Denton slumped over the desk in his study, a bullet hole centered in his chest. The weapon, a World War II pistol from Joshua's gun collection, had been taken from a display cabinet in the Livery entry hall.

"He must've been sitting here working on his stamp collection when someone walked in" deduced the sheriff. "Maybe they had a conversation, maybe not. Anyway, that somebody pulled out a gun and shot him. Simple as pie."

"Maybe not." A deputy was gaping down at a row of stamps scattered across the desktop. "Look. The victim's got a pen in his hand. I was checking to see what he might have been writing and . . ." The deputy pointed to a century-old postage stamp featuring the likeness of Queen Victoria. "You see? He drew a beard on her. A tiny beard and a mustache."

The sheriff frowned. "Why on earth would he do that?"

Whodunit? (1) Who killed Dr. Denton? (2) Why? (3) What was the meaning of the bearded Victoria stamp?

Evidence   *This crime can be solved in 2 clues.*
- Crime Scene Report
- Desktop (Miscellaneous Examinations)
- Poison Analysis (Lab & Hospital Reports)
- $ Joshua Livery's Will (Wills & Insurance)
- Livery Mansion (Miscellaneous Searches)

Swallowing the Gun

May 12, 1:25 P.M.: The police arrive on the scene of what appears to be a grisly suicide. Inside a small, two-story office building lies the body of Hank Bridger, private investigator. Hank had apparently sat down at his desk and shot himself in the mouth. The officers seal the site and then talk to witnesses, beginning with Ethel, the deceased's secretary.

"Hank was out on a case. He came in about noon. I was in his inner office, spraying his plants for bugs. He never takes care of them, and I get tired of looking at the aphids. Anyway, Hank told me to go to lunch and be back by 1:00. Seems he had a lunch appointment of his own at 1:00.

"I had a burger at a fast-food place and did a little window shopping. I was just heading back to the building a few minutes past 1:00. That's when I heard it. Sounded like a truck backfiring. Hank's office is on the first floor; so, it was probably less than 3 minutes from the time I heard the shot until I walked in. When I opened the door to his inner office, I saw him right away, just the way he is now, fallen back in his chair, the gun lying in his hand."

The rest of the story is filled in by another tenant, Blake Barlow, an accountant. "First you have to understand. The four of us own this building. The four tenants are Hank and me on the first floor, Dr. Russell and Milton Engels, a lawyer, on the second. We run the building as a corporation with Hank as the president. Naturally, I do the books.

"Well, recently I ran across something that didn't smell quite right. It looked like one of the corporation members had embezzled quite a decent sum from our escrow fund. Very cleverly embezzled, although I could be wrong. A little past noon today I gave Hank a call. I told him what I'd found. I told him I needed some papers from his safe to check out my suspicions. I said I would drop by to pick them up when I left the office today about 5:00."

Blake gazes down at the body. Hanging on the coat tree by the desk is Hank's empty shoulder holster. Beside it is a paper shredder that had disgorged several sheets of incomprehensible confetti. "I guess that settles it," Blake says. "Hank was the thief. After my call, he opened his safe, destroyed the papers, then sat down and shot himself."

An old lieutenant is taking notes. "Did you tell any of the other partners about your suspicions?"

"No. Just Hank. He said he couldn't believe one of us would do something like that. He even got insulting about my book-keeping. I guess he was trying to bluff me into ignoring it. But I wouldn't. So, he killed himself."

The initial investigation points to the same conclusion. There are no bruises or signs of a struggle. Powder burns on the victim's face support the theory that Hank had opened his mouth willingly, wrapping it around the gun barrel. "Maybe he was asleep in his chair, snoring, and the killer caught him unawares," the lieutenant suggests.

"No," says Ethel. "You see, this office is equipped with an electric-eye alarm system. As soon as someone enters either room, an annoyingly loud bell goes off. That would've woke him instantly. He's a light sleeper. Uh, that's what his wife tells me."

Engels, the lawyer, offers his opinion. "No one in his right mind would sit by while someone took a gun and stuck it into his mouth. Has to be suicide."

The lieutenant shakes his head. "Looks bad, all right. Especially since the rest of you weren't even aware of Mr. Barlow's suspicions. But I knew Hank from his old days on the force. I can't believe he'd steal and I can't believe he'd kill himself. There's got to be another explanation."

Whodunit?   (1) How did the embezzler know he or she was in danger?   (2) Who killed Hank Bridger?   (3) How did the killer manage to shoot Hank in the mouth with his own gun?

Evidence   *This crime can be solved in 3 clues.*
- Crime Scene Report
- Autopsy Report
- *Medical Guide to Poisons* (Research)
- Ethel's Statement (Affidavit File)
- Partners' Alibis (Affidavit File)

The Flighty Freshman

The witness, Bobby McFee, tells his story to the police. "Perry Winkler is a freshman here. Weird guy, a loner. The only reason I know him at all is because sometimes he hangs with the Myers boys. Anyway, I was in the dorm hallway when Perry came up the stairs. It struck me even at the time that he was sneaking in. He kind of jumped when he saw me."

The captain was taking notes. "And you think he came to the dorm specifically to visit Donovan Myers?"

"Yeah. Danny Myers was just coming out of his room. Danny and Donovan are brothers; they room together. Perry asked if Donovan was in. Danny said yes. That's all I saw. I went into my own room at the far end of the hall."

"How much later was it when you saw Perry again?"

"About an hour. They cranked up the stereo, not unusual for a Saturday night. Almost no one else was on the floor, but I have a paper due Monday. I was just coming over to complain about the noise when I saw Perry rushing out of the room and down the stairs. He looked pretty agitated—hair and clothes all messed up. He was carrying a suitcase."

"And your first impulse was to go check on Donovan?"

"Well, the music was still blaring. But, yeah, I guess something didn't seem right. I pushed open the door and there he was on the floor, his head all bashed in. The room looked like a train wreck. I thought Donovan was alive. I mean, his body was still warm. I wouldn't have touched him if I knew."

Captain Mallory understood. "That's okay. Isn't it kind of odd for a loner freshman to be hanging out with big campus jocks like Danny and Donovan? A senior and a junior, right?"

"It is strange. The Myers boys were so outgoing, always pranking around. They're the spoiled kids of a rich family. Lots of friends. I don't think Perry has any friends at all. I guess I've seen him with Donovan a few times and a few times with Danny, but Perry sticks to himself. Back at the start of the year, I remember him being assigned a roommate. That lasted one day. He insisted on a private room. When they wouldn't give him one, he moved off campus."

Mallory finished with the witness, then drove across town

to Perry Winkler's apartment. His men were already on the scene. The suitcase, Donovan's suitcase, lay open and empty on the bed. The rest of Perry's meager possessions seemed intact. "He didn't take much with him," a sergeant said. "But he did leave a note." Using tweezers, the officer held out a letter. "It matches the handwriting from one of his test papers. We're working on the fingerprints now."

The letter was a confession, stating in plain English that he, Perry Winkler, had accidentally killed his friend during a drunken argument over a girl they'd both been dating. "A girl? That doesn't sound like Perry." Mallory scratched his head. "Let's put out an APB for our shy, mysterious killer."

Randall University, although situated in a small town, was a large, impersonal campus, making it easy for a student to get lost in the shuffle. Captain Mallory didn't realize how true this was until he tried to find Perry Winkler. The freshman was distinctive-looking, of regular build and height, but with a mop of frizzy red hair, thick glasses, a bushy mustache, and side-burns.

"We checked everywhere," the sergeant reported two days later. "Perry doesn't own a car which should help us track him down. But no dice. No one answering his description has been spotted at the bus station or hitchhiking out of town. It's like the kid vanished off the face of the earth."

"Something's screwy," Mallory replied. "People don't vanish. It's impossible."

Whodunit?   (1) What happened to Perry Winkler?   (2) Who killed Donovan Myers?   (3) What was the motive?

Evidence   *This crime can be solved in 3 clues.*
- Crime Scene Report
- Perry's School Records (Research)
- Bobby McFee's Testimony (Affidavit File)
- Holographic Results (Miscellaneous Examinations)
- Danny's Testimony (Affidavit File)

Psychic Suicide

"See you next week, Swami. Take care." Pauline Egremont gently closed the door to the shabby room and made her way into the boarding-house kitchen. "I'm a little worried about Swami Fred. He's very depressed today."

The swami's landlady was sitting at the table with Elsie, another one of her boarders. "I bet you'd be depressed, too, Mrs. Egremont," Elsie quipped. "Living in that dumpy room."

The landlady objected. "It's a charming room with direct southern light. Granted, the poor man's a cripple and has his problems, but don't blame it on the room." By problems, the landlady meant the swami's compulsive gambling, a habit that kept him impoverished, despite his affluent clientele.

Mrs. Egremont sniffed a haughty good-bye, leaving the two women to their coffee and chat. About 45 minutes later, according to their testimony, they heard the television go on in the swami's room. Five minutes after that, the psychic's next client showed up.

Noah Turner, a stylishly dressed businessman, muttered hello, marched through the kitchen, and knocked on the swami's door. He tried the knob. It was locked. "He changes my appointment at the last minute and then he's not even here."

"Oh, he must be in," Elsie volunteered. "There's no other door. We would have seen him go out. Hello? Swami Fred? Are you all right?"

The landlady took a set of keys from a peg on the wall. Within seconds she had opened the door, and all three were staring down at the body of Fred Baxter, psychic to society. As always, the tiny man was in his wheelchair. The television droned on as sunlight from the window illuminated a cup of steaming tea on the table by his right hand. A new, freshly lit incense candle tossed its scented smoke into the air. A teakettle simmered on the hot plate, its whistle flipped up and silent.

The landlady gazed at the half-empty cup of tea. "Poison, I'll bet. Must have just done it, too. He'd been depressed lately. That's a fact."

The police confirmed potassium cyanide in the tea. A plastic envelope full of the deadly powder was on the table by the window and bore the deceased's fingerprints.

"What's this?" A rookie cop pointed to an open file cabinet on the far side of the room. The top drawer stood open and totally empty. "I wonder what he was doing?"

A sergeant examining the bathroom came up with the answer. "He was destroying something here in the sink. Muriatic acid," he sniffed. "That's why he used the incense, to get rid of the smell." The sergeant put on plastic gloves and gingerly reached into a large wheelchair-accessible sink. "The contents of that drawer were slipped into this sink and doused with acid." The few remaining fragments, half-eaten edges of paper, were enough to give the sergeant an idea of what had been in the drawer. "Blackmail! Let's talk to the landlady."

The landlady was reluctant to pass along the idle gossip of a boarding house, but Elsie wasn't. "We figured he had another income source. I mean, he lost so much. His bookie actually brags about it, and it stands to reason a psychic would blackmail people. Even if he's a phony, clients wind up telling him all sorts of things about themselves."

The rookie glanced over his notes and announced his theory. "A clear case of suicide. Even with blackmail, he's a handicapped guy in debt and depressed. So, he locks the door, clears out his files—his one decent act—puts on incense to get rid of the smell, and drinks a cupful of cyanide. It all fits."

"Not quite." The sergeant tapped his finger on the just completed inventory list. "There's something missing. I mean, an actual, physical thing missing from this room. And that tells me it's murder we're dealing with, not suicide."

Whodunit?   (1) Who killed Swami Fred Baxter?   (2) How was it done?

Evidence   *This case can be solved in 2 clues.*
- ⚷ Autopsy Report
- 🔫 Behind House (Miscellaneous Searches)
- 👤 Noah Turner's Statement (Affidavit File)
- 🐾 Crime Scene Report
- 👤 Landlady's Statement (Affidavit File)

Accidents Will Happen

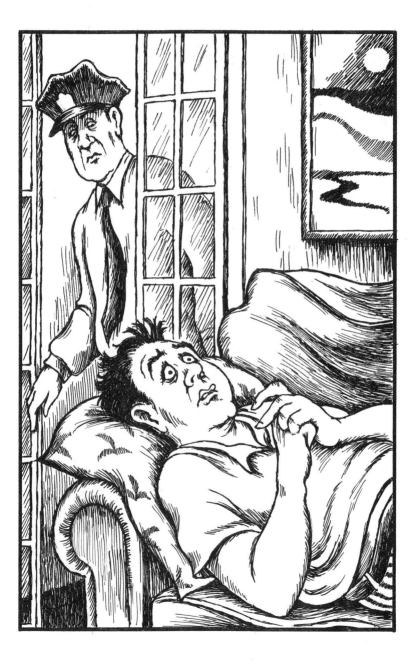

"Hi, Mr. Cullen? I've made up my mind, just this minute while I'm heading to work. I want to testify. Not that I know that much. Sal didn't introduce me to many people. But it should be enough to put a few of them behind bars."

Special Agent Cullen nearly dropped the phone. For the past 4 months, he'd been trying to talk Lana Salvatore into telling the FBI what she knew her ex-husband and the Boitano crime family. "I want you to come into my office."

"I'm on my way right now."

"What? You're calling from a car phone?" Cullen started to sweat. "Those things aren't safe. I want you to drive straight here. Don't stop anywhere. Don't call anyone else. I'll meet you out front."

Lana laughed. "Don't worry. I've taken my own precautions. Be there in 20 minutes."

An hour later Cullen got the report from highway patrol. Lana Salvatore's compact coupe had been found off the side of a country road. It had broken through a wooden guardrail, plummeted down a ravine, and smashed headlong into a massive oak. Ten minutes after Lana's call, a local farmer heard the crash. He discovered her behind the wheel, not wearing a safety belt. The driver's side air bag had inflated but it wasn't enough to save her. By the time the ambulance arrived, the would-be witness was dead from massive internal injuries.

Cullen rejected the highway patrol's assumption of accidental death and went in search of Sal Salvatore, Lana's "ex." The cement company executive had his alibi ready and waiting. "At 8:00 this morning? Sure. I just got off a plane. Business trip. I was driving in from the airport on the other side of town. Check with my boss, Mr. Boitano. At a few minutes past 8:00, I was on my car phone calling into the office. Here's my plane ticket and I'm sure the phone company has a record of the call."

Big Tony Boitano also had an alibi. "I was in the office, like Sal said. We was having a board meeting. Sal called in and I put him on the speaker. A dozen of my guys can swear I was there and Sal was on the phone. How many times I gotta tell you jerks—I run a legitimate cement company here."

The last interview on Cullen's list was Pauly Adidas, Lana's boyfriend. He found the young man on a couch in their living room, appearing pale and in great emotional pain. "We just got engaged," he whispered. "She drove off this morning while I was still in bed. I tell you, if I'd known what she was up to I would've stopped her. You don't mess with killers."

Agent Cullen grew discouraged. Even if the mob had overheard Lana's cellular call, how could they have intercepted her car so quickly and forced it off the road? He was almost ready to admit defeat when, that same evening, he got word from the police of a break-in at Lana's house. The dead woman's fiancé fended them off but had been severely beaten in the process, suffering broken ribs.

Pauly gave a statement from the hospital emergency room. "My car's in the shop, so I guess they thought the house was empty. I was watching TV when I heard glass breaking down in the living room. There were two of them wearing masks. I grabbed a baseball bat, but they're a lot more used to fighting than me. The neighbors heard all the noise and called the police." Unfortunately, the neighbors never actually saw the intruders, and Pauly couldn't provide a description any more detailed than that they were large and male.

The FBI agent pondered the information, then smiled. "We've still got a chance. If they broke into her house, it means they were looking for something they wanted. Maybe a diary naming names. This case isn't over yet."

Whodunit?   (1) What's the story behind Pauly's attack and injuries?   (2) Who killed Lana?   (3) How was the murder committed?

Evidence   *This case can be solved in 2 clues.*
- Crime Scene Report
- Autopsy Report
- Pauly's Hospital Report (Lab & Hospital Reports)
- Farmer's Statement (Affidavit File)
- Area near Crash Site (Miscellaneous Searches)

Gunfight at the O.K. Motel

Jack Bosco entered the O.K. Motel office to settle his phone charges and return the key. "You see it on the news? Two guys just robbed a bank here in town and drove off with a million in cash. I guess they'll catch 'em. They got the roads blocked."

The motel manager grunted and printed out a receipt. He watched as the burly traveling salesman walked out the door, nearly colliding with two men who were just coming inside to register. The newcomers said little, kept their heads down, and seemed in a hurry to get a room, even though it was only 11:30 A.M.

At high noon, the shot rang out, a single gunshot. Since only one unit was occupied, the manager didn't have any trouble telling the 911 operator where to send the police.

The responding officer recognized the car in the motel lot from the APB and called for backup. Within minutes six patrol cars were on the scene, and a captain was shouting through a bullhorn. "Police! You're under arrest. Open the door slowly. Throw out your weapons and come out . . ." Before he could finish, a figure at the picture window broke the glass and sprayed the lot with a spurt of semiautomatic fire.

Twelve officers shot back. Over the next few minutes, they fired dozens of rounds until the shadowy form by the corner of the window no longer seemed to be there. "I don't think he's fired since our first response," the captain mumbled to his lieutenant. "Maybe we should go in."

When they broke down the door, the police found one of the robbers on the floor, dead. A volley of bullets had knocked him off a chair positioned by the window. "Stupid. He should have given up or hid himself better." The captain stepped around to the other side of the bed. That's when he discovered the second body on the rug, lying on its side facing the bed.

The burly figure had been gagged and loosely tied with sash cords cut down from the blinds. The motel manager identified him as Jack Bosco, the salesman who had checked out just moments before the bank robbers checked in.

The captain examined the cords and shook his head. "Not very good with knots." He looked at the single bullet wound and shook his head again. "Why the heck would they do this? What's the point of having a hostage if you kill him right off?"

The second bank robber was caught a short time later trying to steal a car from a nearby auto dealership. "After we checked in," he said, "I ran across to the market for food and cigarettes. I didn't take the car, just in case there was a description out. 'Course I didn't know they were plastering the t.v. with the bank's video of our faces and the car and everything else. When I left Buddy, we didn't have a hostage or anything. Honest. All I know is when I come out of the market there's a parking lot full of cops shooting up the place. So I just ran."

"Where's the rest of the money?" the captain snapped.

"What rest of the money? It's all in the room. Four big bags of it."

"No, it's not. Only two bags are there. What did you do with the other two?"

"Honest. I just went to the store. A half-hour later, there's a shoot-out and a dead hostage and half the money gone? I don't know what happened."

A short time later the police discovered the whereabouts of the missing bags.

Whodunit?   (1) What happened in the motel room? (2) How did half of the money end up where it did? (3) Who killed Jack Bosco?

Evidence   *This case can be solved in 3 clues.*
- ⚕ Buddy's Autopsy Report
- ⚕ Jack Bosco's Autopsy Report
- 🔫 Jack's Car (Miscellaneous Searches)
- 🐾 Crime Scene Report
- 🏠 Investigation of Jack's Past (Research)

The Show Girl Murders

"She was already dead when I got there," Tim Gleason stammered to the police. The teenager had bluffed his way backstage only to find himself embroiled in a murder.

"I've seen the show a dozen times. I wanted to meet the actors, so I told the stage doorman I was the leading lady's son just home from school. He pointed me back toward her dressing room. I could hear them rehearsing onstage. Almost no one was backstage, just two show girls. I passed by this side hall and saw them standing by the fire extinguisher talking. I'm not sure they saw me. It was pretty quick."

The young fan said he had just reached the end of the corridor when he heard the scream. "It came from the top of this spiral staircase. I ran up the stairs. There was only one door in sight. I knocked a couple of times and heard some noise inside. Finally I pushed it open and there she was."

Dolly Lawson had been thrown across the makeup table, her dressing gown open provocatively and her head smashed into the mirror. A dagger-like shard of glass was lodged deep in her throat. "The side door was open and I sort of heard someone running down the spiral stairs. I should've gone to see who it was, but I was stunned. I'd never seen a dead person."

The homicide detective checked Tim's story with the stage doorman and with Dora, one of the two surviving show girls. "He saw Deedee and me standing in the side hall?" She frowned and adjusted her elbow-length gloves. "Oh, yeah. A young guy walked by, about 15 feet away. It was just a few seconds after that when we heard the scream. Poor Dolly."

Based on this corroboration, the police let Tim go, warning him to remain available for further questioning. The detective next turned his attention to the cast. The director gathered them together in the green room and presented their collective alibi.

"We were in the middle of a brush-up. Everyone was onstage, except the show girls. The only other people in the house were the pianist down in the pit and a lighting technician. He was in the wings, pulling the light cues for the musical number we were rehearsing. Oh, and Johnny, the doorman. He was in his office by the door."

"You're telling me no one else was in the theater? Then how did Miss Lawson get killed? Maybe she banged her own head into the mirror and committed suicide?" Reluctantly, the detective let the cast go and focused his investigation on the others, trying to find a chink in their alibis. He had just finished questioning the pianist and was beginning with the lighting man when a second scream, even more gut-wrenching than the first, echoed through the old Broadway house.

They found Deedee Adams backstage in a narrow walkway behind a section of the finale set. One of the spears from the voodoo number had been shoved between the beads in her skimpy costume, skewering her right through the stomach.

They barely had time to check for a pulse before another noise caught their attention. A shattering crash of glass led them to a side corridor where the broken remnants of a full-length mirror lay scattered across the floor. The pianist scratched his head. "Two murders. Two broken mirrors."

"He's going to get me next, I know it." Dora, the one re-maining show girl, was in a panic. "It's a maniac. Some sick, puritanical maniac is killing off show girls."

The homicide detective gazed at the shivering woman. In her costume, she looked nearly identical to the latest victim. "Well, it does look like a pattern," he agreed, perhaps a bit injudiciously.

Whodunit? (1) Who killed Dolly and why? (2) Who killed Deedee and why? (3) Why was the hall mirror broken?

Evidence *This crime can be solved in 3 clues.*
- ♟ Doorman's Testimony (Affidavit File)
- ♀ Dolly's Autopsy Report
- ✍ Crime Scene Report (Dolly's Dressing Room)
- ◈ Broken Mirror (Miscellaneous Examinations)
- ♟ Tim's Testimony (Affidavit File)

Manny, Moe, or Jack

It was a blustery morning in late fall when Adolph Prep sat his sons down in the breakfast room of his country mansion and announced the news. "Just thought you should know. The lawyer's on his way. I'm changing my will today and you're all out. The money will go to Charity."

Manny, the eldest, choked on his Colombian coffee. "You can't do this. All our lives we've been . . . Dadums, please. You were never interested in charitable stuff."

"Who said anything about . . . I mean Charity, my housekeeper. We've grown close since you boys have been on your own living it up." And without stopping to listen to the pleas from his sniveling offspring, the cantankerous millionaire rose from the table and hobbled up the stairs to his room.

Crimson with rage, Manny sprinted for the privacy of the library telephone. "He can't do this. I have debts. My lawyer will know what to do."

Jack, the youngest, headed for the gun cabinet, whistled for the dog, and grabbed a rifle. "I hope I find something to shoot. That's the only thing that'll calm me down."

Of the three Prep boys, Moe, the middle son, seemed to take it the best. He spent a half hour stoking the six downstairs fireplaces, then headed upstairs to talk to the old man. "I'm sure he didn't mean it. Just trying to get a rise out of us."

Ten minutes later, he came down, disappointed. "He's really serious," Moe told his older brother. "We have to do something. His lawyer's coming in an hour. What did *your* lawyer say?"

"He says there's nothing we can do." Manny lowered the receiver. "Maybe if I talk to the old monster . . ."

Moe watched from the library as Manny climbed the stairs. He stood there transfixed as the wood snapped and popped in the fireplace. And then suddenly one pop seemed louder than the others. Louder and from a different location. "Manny! What are you doing? Charity!"

Moe and the young housekeeper reached the top of the stairs at the same time. The corridor was dim, but light was streaming out from under one of the closed doors. They saw

Manny kneeling in front of this door, his eye at keyhole level. He turned to face them. "I can't see a thing."

Charity fumbled for her key ring. Seconds later the three of them were staring into Adolph Prep's private sanctum. The millionaire was on the bed lying on his back with his legs dangling over the edge, a .38-caliber pistol lying in his palm. A surprisingly tiny blob of red stained his shirt with a little black hole centered just over his heart.

Despite the fire roaring merrily in the grate, the room was unexpectedly cold. In a moment, they saw why. A set of French windows faced onto a small balcony. One of the middle panes had been shattered and the wind whistled in from the green lawn and the woods beyond.

"What's going on?" Jack Prep stood in the bedroom doorway, still dressed for hunting, his rifle tucked under his arm. "I was coming back across the lawn. I happened to look up at Dad's room. Then all of a sudden I heard this shot and glass breaking. Someone shot out Dad's window."

Jack glanced at the body, then up at his smiling brothers, then at the accusing frown of the housekeeper. "Hey! What're you staring at? I didn't kill him. My gun hasn't been fired. You can smell the barrel. He must have committed suicide."

"Oh, I can smell something all right," Charity snarled. "And it's not suicide."

Whodunit?   (1) Who killed Adolph Prep?   (2) How was it done?

Evidence   *This case can be solved in 3 clues.*
- ♰   Autopsy Report
- ⌐   Outside Bedroom Window (Miscellaneous Searches)
- ⌐   Behind Bedroom Bureau (Miscellaneous Searches)
- ⌐   Bedroom Fireplace (Miscellaneous Searches)
- ☞   Crime Scene Report

The Phantom Intruder

Chef Teddy Gouda had just ushered out the last of his customers and was locking up. "We'll do the cleanup in the morning," he informed his wife. "I'm going to bed."

"Is anything the matter?" Esther asked gently. Chef Teddy had been moodier than usual lately. When he wasn't taking care of business in their small country restaurant, he was almost always off by himself, playing with his chocolate labrador retriever in the woods out back.

"The matter?" He snorted and headed upstairs to their living quarters. "You should know what the matter is; you and my no-good partner should know better than anyone!"

Esther sighed and followed her husband up the stairs. She was used to his jealousies; there was no point arguing.

Somewhere in the middle of the night, Teddy shook his wife awake. "Did you hear that? Someone is downstairs. A burglar."

"It's your imagination," Esther yawned. "Hershey isn't barking. Go back to sleep." But Teddy was already up, slipping on his bathrobe, and heading out into the hall.

Esther sat up in bed. She could hear him shuffling down the hall. A minute later, she heard him somewhere downstairs in the back of the restaurant, his voice raised in anger. "Esterbrook!" he barked. "What are you doing here? What do you mean . . . Put that down!" Then a single, deafening gunshot erupted in the still night air.

When the sheriff arrived on the scene, he found the body of Teddy Gouda on the floor of the rear dining room, shot once in the head from close range. The French doors stood open, giving access to the dark woods beyond. There was no weapon in sight.

Oscar, Teddy's elderly father, had also been upstairs and confirmed Esther's story. "It was about 2 o'clock when Teddy came and woke me up. He said someone had broken in and he was going to check it out. After he left, I got worried and followed him downstairs. His voice was coming from the rear dining room. It couldn't have been more than 15 seconds after the gunshot when I ran in there. The French doors were still swinging. I could hear the crunch of leaves and branches, like someone running through the woods, but it was too dark to see."

Emma Cook, the restaurant's only neighbor, corroborated the sequence of events. "I was awake at 2 A.M. Couldn't sleep. From my bed I could see the lights in their rear dining room. The French doors were slightly ajar. About 10 seconds after the shot, they banged open. Someone or something was racing out of the room and into the woods."

"Things look pretty bad for this Esterbrook." Sheriff Mugs checked his notes. "The guy is Gouda's business partner and he was carrying on with Gouda's wife, allegedly. And two witnesses swear the victim called out his name right before the gunshot." The sheriff was just about to issue an arrest order when Paul Esterbrook himself walked through the door.

The young businessman didn't seem at all nervous and had his own story to tell. "Teddy called me yesterday. He asked me to meet him at the restaurant at 2 A.M. Something secret he couldn't discuss over the phone. He insisted on 2 A.M. exactly and I couldn't talk him out of it. Well, as it happened, I was running a bit late. Lucky for me. One of your deputies stopped me for speeding. Look here at the ticket, 2:05 A.M. I was standing by my car, two miles away, when the 911 came in over his radio."

The sheriff bit his lip and cursed. "I hate it when my best suspect has an alibi. I hate it even more when he gets it from one of my own men."

Whodunit?   (1) Who killed Chef Teddy?   (2) How was it done?   (3) What happened to the murder weapon?

Evidence   *This case can be solved in 3 clues.*
- ⚕ Autopsy Report
- 🔫 Teddy and Esther's Bedroom (Miscellaneous Searches)
- 🐕 Experiment with Barking Dog (Research)
- 🔫 Woods (Miscellaneous Searches)
- $ Wills & Insurance

Shot in the Cul-de-Sac

Ollie West glowered across the suburban lawns to one of the houses on the neighboring cul-de-sac. "Every day Ms. Peterson's dog escapes from her yard. It digs up my flower beds, not to mention the poop it leaves. I want you to impound it or arrest her. I've had enough."

This was the third time the officer had responded to West's complaints. Didn't he know there were more important crimes, even here in the 'burbs? Then, as if to prove the officer's point, a frightened shout was heard in the distance. A man's voice. Then a shot. Moments later, a second gunshot. "One of the houses over there," the homeowner said, pointing to the same cul-de-sac. "I hope it's the dog."

There were three residences on the dead-end street, two of which had cars in the drives. The young officer had never responded to a shooting before. Nervously, he approached the first house. When no one responded to his knocks, he sneaked a peek through the adjacent window. A dead body lay spread-eagle by the couch.

After calling for the homicide boys, the rookie made a tour of the perimeter and found the kitchen door unlocked. Inside, all seemed normal, except for the smell of gunpowder, a broken mug on the floor, and two sets of footprints trailing through the spilled coffee and into the living room. The officer touched nothing. The victim, a man, was dressed in a bathrobe with a bullethole in the back and a ribbon of red trickling down. According to the mail on the end table, this might be Edward D. Smucker, who "might already be a sweepstakes winner."

The assistant medical examiner was the first to arrive. She had been listening in on the police band and happened to be nearby, even though this was her day off. She sent the rookie outside to wait for the others, then set about her investigation.

The police soon had a rough idea of what they were dealing with. The victim was indeed Ed Smucker, a writer working out of his home. The on-site evidence indicated that he had been drinking a cup of coffee in his kitchen when someone entered the house through the kitchen door. The attacker chased him into the living room, firing a wild shot into the doorjamb before hitting Ed squarely in the back.

The victim's wife, Marlene, a lawyer who worked in the city, had been on her way home, an hour-long commute, at the time of the murder. The body had just been removed when Marlene pulled into the drive. She collapsed on the lawn, hysterical with shock and grief, behavior that surprised the neighbors, who had grown used to the Smuckers' domestic disputes.

That same night, while Marlene stayed with a friend, the rookie was on duty again, making sure that no one disturbed the crime-scene tape plastered over the doors and windows. It was nearly 2 A.M. when he heard another gunshot, this one coming from the woods that lay between the development and the highway. The lights went on in a few nearby houses, and before the officer knew it, Ollie West was walking up to his patrol car. "Let's go check it out," Ollie suggested. The rookie was reluctant to leave his post but even more reluctant to let Ollie go back there alone. Together, the two men took flashlights into the woods but were unable to find anyone or anything out of the ordinary. On their return, the officer sighed in relief to see that none of the tapes had been disturbed.

Before Ollie went home, he made an interesting observation. "These people with their guns. I mean, how are they getting into the area? It's a quiet neighborhood. I certainly haven't seen any cars hanging around, or people for that matter. It's strange."

The rookie nodded. "I have a feeling it's going to get a lot stranger before it's over. Mark my words."

Whodunit?   (1) Who killed Ed Smucker?   (2) Why?   (3) How was the murder committed?

Evidence   *This case can be solved in 3 clues.*
- Autopsy Report
- Bedroom (Miscellaneous Searches)
- Crime Scene Report
- Woods (Miscellaneous Searches)
- Ballistics Test (Lab & Hospital Reports)

How the Other Half Dies

Bryce Carlton looked out of place in the dingy station house as he filled out a Missing Persons form. "I last saw my sister Friday night," the millionaire playboy told the female officer. It was now noon on Monday. "We went to this new restaurant on the other side of town to meet some friends. Tracy and I got there early and had a drink. As usual, we got into a fight—about money. Tracy caused a scene and just stormed out. I should have followed her, but I didn't."

"And that's the last you saw of her? Friday night?"

Bryce looked embarrassed. "Our friends arrived about 8:00. We had dinner, then we hopped in my car to go out to my beach house. Tracy was supposed to join us. She never came back to the restaurant; so, we went without her. Tracy can be stubborn. I'm her guardian until she turns 21 next year. She doesn't like the fact that I control her money."

"Did you hear from her at all during the weekend?"

"I tried calling the penthouse but she wasn't in. Saturday morning she phoned the beach house. She said she was spending the weekend with a friend. When I asked what friend, she got mad and hung up. This morning I came back into town. Tracy wasn't at the penthouse and none of her friends had seen her. That's when I came to you."

The officer was about to dole out some words of comfort when the news came in. Tracy's body had been pulled out of the river. It had floated to the surface within the grounds of the family tannery, Carlton Leather, about a mile from the restaurant where she'd last been seen. She'd been shot once in the head, and a preliminary autopsy placed the time of death as sometime Sunday evening. Since the tannery had been closed for the weekend, it was assumed that the killer gained entry through an unguarded side gate.

The police began their investigation with Tracy's boyfriend, Clyde Olmsted, a young man who worked at the tannery. The last time he'd seen Tracy, he said, was Friday afternoon when she dropped by work to tell him she couldn't see him that weekend. "Her brother had talked her into going to the beach house. Of course, I'm not welcome there. Bryce wouldn't even let me have dinner with them Friday night. He didn't approve of me. If Tracy changed her mind about going away, I don't know why she didn't call me. I just hung around by myself most of the weekend. Doing laundry, that sort of thing."

Gina Tadburn, the dead girl's best friend, came next. "Tracy wouldn't have gone to see Clyde. She was tired of him. They were on the verge of breaking up, whether he knew it or not. Something must have happened after she left the restaurant. Otherwise she would have called me. I can't see her spending a weekend alone, that's for sure."

Both Gina and Clyde mentioned the victim's only enemy, Anna Hart. Anna was Bryce's fiancée. The millionaire's sister and his future wife never got along and had been known to engage in fistfights. Since both women were roughly the same height and weight, their brawls usually ended in a draw.

Anna was quick to volunteer her alibi. "I didn't join them at the restaurant because I wanted to get Bryce's beach house ready for the guests. I drove out Friday night and got there about two hours before the others. The house is an hour and a half from the city, and I don't think any of us was alone for more than an hour at a time. Not for the entire weekend."

The police checked with hospitals, hotels, and any other accommodations within a 100-mile radius. The results were pure frustration. No one had seen Tracy from the time she stormed out of the restaurant to her estimated time of death on Sunday. "Where was she for nearly two days?" the homicide chief wondered. "Young heiresses just don't vanish."

Whodunit?　(1) Where did Tracy spend the weekend? (2) Who killed her?　(3) How was the murder covered up?

Evidence　*This case can be solved in 3 clues.*
- Crime Scene Report
- Waitress's Testimony (Affidavit File)
- Telephone Records (Research)
- Maid's Testimony (Affidavit File)
- Test Water Sample (Lab & Hospital Reports)

Daylight Saving Crime

"I think they killed him." The tiny clergyman peered up at the desk sergeant. "He's one of my parishioners, Richie Okan. There's a lot of bad blood between him and his brother, Phil. Also, I know that Phil and Richie's wife are closer than in-laws should be. Anyway, all three took off on Richie's boat today. When they came back, Richie wasn't with them and they were acting odd. That made me suspicious." The Rev. Cal Brown was well respected; so, the police thought it best to do a little checking.

Linda Okan was brought in for questioning and quickly broke down—in return for immunity. "Yes, Phil and I are in love. We didn't think Richie knew, but I guess that minister clued him in. Today the three of us went for a picnic on Palmetto Island. Richie and Phil got into a fight. They're both big men and, well . . . A bread knife wound up in Richie's stomach. Phil panicked. He said no one would believe it was self-defense. We buried Richie there on the island, then made up a story about dropping him off at Crown Bay."

Phil's story was quite different. "Linda and I aren't in love and I certainly didn't kill my brother. We built a fire on the island, had our picnic, then headed back home. Richie asked us to drop him at a pier near Crown Bay. He said he wanted to visit friends." The friends in question swore that Richie did not visit them.

The next day, Sunday, the police took Linda to Palmetto Island, where she pointed to a shallow grave. When they dug, however, all they found were a pile of ashes, some trash from the picnic, a ring and a belt buckle, both belonging to Richie. The captain was outraged. "How could Phil move the body? We've been keeping track of him ever since Mrs. Okan came in for questioning."

A rookie cop meekly offered an explanation. "I was on surveillance last night at his house. I had a view of both the street and the beach. When 2 o'clock rolled around and Groff wasn't there to replace me . . . Well, I figured he was running a minute late. I left. I didn't realize that Saturday night was the change-over from daylight saving time. When the clock struck 2:00, it was suddenly 1 o'clock again. No one was surveilling Phil Okan for almost an hour."

Officer Groff came to the rookie's defense. "Give the kid a break, Captain. Okan didn't go anywhere. He's got no boat and he sure didn't swim out to Palmetto Island. Two miles? In the middle of the night? As soon as I got to Okan's house, I checked the windows. He was in the living room watching t.v. Fifty-five minutes at the max. What could he have done in 55 minutes? That corpse'll show up. Don't worry."

On Tuesday, the corpse did show up. A thunderstorm raged that morning and lightning struck an abandoned shack near Crown Bay. When the fire department arrived on the scene, they stumbled across the charred remains of Richie Okan.

The clerk at a convenience store not far from the shack told his story. "It was late Saturday night. Some big guy with a beard came in to buy cold cuts. The beard was real fake. Anyway, he walked off in the direction of the shack." When shown a picture of Phil Okan, the clerk could not make a positive identification.

The captain was fuming. "How could he dig up the body, move it to Crown Bay, and get back in 55 minutes? And without a boat. It's impossible."

Whodunit?   (1) Who killed Richie Okan?   (2) Why?   (3) How did the body wind up in an abandoned shack?

Evidence   *This case can be solved in 3 clues.*
- ♟ Linda's Testimony (Affidavit File)
- $ Richie's Estate (Wills & Insurance)
- ⌐ Coast near Beach House (Miscellaneous Searches)
- ✍ Crime Scene Report
- ⚕ Autopsy Report

Last of the Royal Blood

The limousine pulled through the gates. The three passengers gazed out at the guards with their dogs patrolling the imposing estate. "Cool," Mary Ann whispered. "You become pals with some dude on the Net and you've got no idea that he's really some deposed Middle Eastern shah."

Mary Ann, Chuck, and Rodney were, like the Shah of Ibabi, all in their midtwenties. All four had become friends on the Internet, but they hadn't thought of meeting until the shah revealed his identity and asked them to visit his home-in-exile on the shores of a Vermont lake. They met for the first time at the airport when the shah's driver picked them up.

It had been a nearly snowless winter, but the air was still bitterly cold. Rodney pressed his nose to the frosty glass as the mansion came into view. "Poor guy. Parents dead. Stuck out in the boonies with nothing but a male entourage. No wonder he invited us to celebrate his birthday."

Chuck scratched his head. "Why do you suppose he keeps his birthday a secret?"

"I don't think it's a secret. He just maintains a low profile. You know. Keep himself out of the papers, that sort of thing. He's got political enemies. You guys both bought him a nice present, I hope. Like we talked about?" Rodney asked.

Ali, the shah's chief aide, met them at the door and led them into the grand hall, a room richly decorated, with hundreds of reminders of the owner's desert home. "Thank you for coming. His Majesty looks forward to meeting you. In the meantime, please make yourselves at home." For the rest of the afternoon, they settled into their rooms, recovering from their flights and roaming the eerily deserted mansion.

The shah was overjoyed to meet his electronic pen pals. But even though they had logged on hundreds of hours with him, they felt ill at ease and spent much of the dinner asking about his former kingdom. For dessert Ali brought in a cake, and the three guests unveiled their presents.

Chuck had brought a gift pack featuring delicacies from his home state. "You always ask me about Utah; so, I thought I'd bring you a few things."

Rodney's present was wrapped in leftover Christmas paper. "It's the best book on surfing the Internet," he explained, a little embarrassed by his makeshift packaging.

Mary Ann's gift was tied in paisley silk, pulled through a gold ring at the top. "It's an Ibabi antique I found in a shop, though I don't suppose you need any more."

The shah unwrapped a small iron statue with a square base. "No, no. This is beautiful. Thank you." He put down his last present, then gazed out at the frozen lake and the lights of the quaint village on the far shore. "It means much to me to finally have friends here. Tomorrow we will talk." And sadly, the young former ruler left the table and headed up to his room.

That night, Ali couldn't sleep. They had never had strangers in this house, and although a security firm had checked their backgrounds, he still felt uneasy. At a few minutes past midnight, the aide walked by the shah's room, tried the knob, and found it unlocked. "Your Majesty?" He opened the door.

The Shah of Ibabi lay faceup across the rug, the handle of an ornamental dagger sticking out of his chest. Ali raced over to the button by the bed and sounded the alarm. A dozen deadbolts flew into place and the mansion was sealed off.

Although it was late, none of the guests were in their rooms. Ali tracked them down and gathered them together in the grand hall. The security director had already phoned the police. In the meanwhile, Ali was determined to find the killer and administer his own kind of justice. He figured he had at least half an hour before the American authorities arrived and took over. He had to move fast.

Whodunit?   (1) Who killed the Shah of Ibabi?   (2) Why? (3) How was the killer planning to get away?

Evidence   *This case can be solved in 2 clues.*
- ⌐ Grand Hall (Miscellaneous Searches)
- ⌐ Mud Room (Miscellaneous Searches)
- ✍ Crime Scene Report
- 🕵 Guests' Alibis (Affidavit File)
- ◎ Guests' Luggage (Miscellaneous Examinations)

🕵 Affidavit File

Accidents Will Happen (Farmer's Testimony)
The farmer who discovered the accident says he was in the shower at the time. "I was home sick. Otherwise, I would've been in the fields with my sons. I heard this crash. No squeal of tires, just a loud metallic crash. It took me no more than a few minutes to get dressed and outside. Right away I saw the broken guardrail and the car smacked against the tree. There were no cars or other people in sight."

Checking Out (Scotty's Testimony)
The young waiter was interviewed the following day while changing into his white shirt and regulation brown bow tie. "Mr. Williams phoned in his order at 3:12 P.M., that's what his ticket says. Salad, a rare steak, fries, and a beer. The kitchen wasn't busy, so it was ready to take up at about 3:35. Is that all? My shift is about to start and I don't want to be late."

Daylight Saving Crime (Linda's Testimony)
When we got back, we docked the boat, then went into a nearby bar. We were pretty shaken up. Phil said he wanted to borrow Richie's jet ski, just in case he needed it. We waited until nobody was in sight, then we went to our slip and lifted it into the back of Phil's pickup. Phil took me home, then drove

off with the jet ski." There were no witnesses at the dock to verify this. No one noticed exactly when Richie Okan's jet ski disappeared.

The Flighty Freshman (Bobby McFee's Testimony)
In a second interview, Bobby McFee added several details. When he saw Perry that night in the dorm, the freshman didn't look at all drunk. On the other hand, Danny Myers appeared quite intoxicated.

Bobby couldn't recall Perry ever having been out with a girl. Donovan's girlfriend was Alicia Henderson. Last year Alicia had been dating Danny, but early this semester they broke up and Alicia began dating Donovan.

The Flighty Freshman (Danny's Testimony)
In a sworn statement, Danny Myers says he left the dorm floor just as Perry was arriving. He went directly to Alicia Henderson's apartment, arriving at least half an hour before Bobby McFee discovered the murder. Alicia was a former girlfriend of Danny's and had recently begun dating his brother. Alicia confirms Danny's alibi, saying they'd been together in her apartment studying for a biology exam until a friend telephoned to inform them of Donovan's death.

How the Other Half Dies (Waitress's Testimony)
A cocktail waitress recalled Tracy's presence Friday night. "How could I forget? She made such a scene. They got here about 7:30. She was in this great brown dress with a very dramatic hat, like out of an old movie. They weren't here 5 minutes before they got into a fight. It was pretty embarrassing. The owner was just about to come over when she got up and left. It looked like the brother was going to go after her, but he didn't. He just sat there and ordered another two drinks. Then his friends showed up for dinner."

How the Other Half Dies (Maid's Testimony)
The Carlton maid talked about the last time she saw Tracy.

"They were fighting about everything. Which dress should she wear, the beige or the brown? Should she wear a hat? How early should they leave for the restaurant? Should they go someplace for drinks first? They were still arguing when they left. About 6:15. I think Miss Tracy stuck to her guns. Beige. No hat. And they settled on going someplace for drinks."

Last of the Royal Blood (Guests' Alibis)
According to their statements and the testimony of the servants, the guests had been in these locations at the time they were informed of the shah's murder.

Rodney: In the rose garden, getting a little fresh air. The small garden directly behind the mansion is the only part of the grounds safe from the guards and their dogs.

Chuck: On the roof above the tower room, the shah had installed a telescope. Chuck was here on the mansion roof, looking at the stars.

Mary Ann: In the first-floor kitchen, in search of a midnight snack.

Psychic Suicide (Noah Turner's Statement)
Noah Turner had a session with Swami Fred every Friday at noon. This morning, however, Noah says he received a phone call from a woman claiming to be the swami's assistant, changing his appointment from noon to 1 P.M. He didn't recognize the voice. A search warrant reveals that at the time the body was discovered, Noah was carrying $2,000 in cash in a plain envelope. He insists it's petty cash from his business.

Psychic Suicide (Landlady's Statement)
The landlady says that both Pauline Egremont and Noah Turner are regular clients, Pauline at 11:00 every Friday and Noah at noon. She is also willing to swear that no one could have entered the swami's room from the time Pauline left to the time Noah arrived. "Oops! Not quite true. I remember

now. Shortly after Mrs. Egremont left, I took a potty break. But Elsie was in the kitchen while I was gone. She says no one went in his room. You can trust her."

The Show Girl Murders (Tim's Testimony)
Tim responded when questioned over telephone: "I don't know anything about that second mirror or why it was broken. I didn't see any mirror. The only fire extinguisher I remember was in the side hall beside where the show girls were standing. There was no mirror there."

The Show Girl Murders (Doorman's Testimony)
"Personally, I'd put my money on Max Lumen, the lighting guy. Everyone knows he was carrying on with Dolly, the first victim. Real hot and heavy. Then yesterday I heard him bragging to the stagehands about how he was fooling around with another show girl here. I figure Dolly got wind of it. The lady had a temper. Max and her fought and she accidentally got killed. Deedee was the other show girl involved and when she figured out what happened, he had to kill her, too."

Swallowing the Gun (Partners' Alibis)
All three of Hank's partners claimed to have been alone in their offices between 12:30 P.M. and the time of the shot. The doctor's nurse and the lawyer's secretary went out to lunch together at noon. Barlow himself had recently fired his secretary and not yet replaced her. Occasionally, the partners joined each other for lunch, but today all three claimed to be alone in their offices. Telephone records verify Barlow's call to the deceased at 12:09 P.M.

Swallowing the Gun (Ethel's Statement)
Under intense questioning, Ethel admitted to having an affair with the deceased. "Just a fling last fall. We saw each other for a month and it ended by mutual consent. I half expected him to fire me, but we managed to maintain a working relationship."

Ethel's alibi is corroborated by the two other women working in the building. While window shopping, Ethel ran into the lawyer's secretary and the doctor's nurse. The three of them walked back to the building and were together when they heard the gunshot.

Video Violence (Fred Fleer's Testimony)
Fred describes the intruder as wearing tight-fitting camouflage fatigues. Other than the fit, his memory of the assailant jibes with Gregory's. When asked about Jane Jones's connection to "Exposé," he says: "Jane was executive producer. Renaldo did it for tax purposes, putting his part of the company in her name. I guess that's why the Mob included her in the hit. I'm in charge of day-to-day production."

Fred's alibi seems to check out. He had been on the phone for about 20 minutes. His assistant on the other end swears that she heard the gunshot in the distance.

☤ Autopsy Reports

Accidents Will Happen
Death was caused by massive internal injuries, trauma, and loss of blood. In addition, the right clavicle had been snapped in a compound fracture.

Note: The deceased was wearing makeup, but only part of it appears to have been applied. The lower lip, for example, was free of lipstick.

Checking Out
Body discovered at 3:40 P.M. M.E. arrived at 4:18 P.M. and began examination. A human body cools at approximately 3 degrees an hour; so, it can be deduced that death occurred between 3:00 and 3:20 P.M.

Cause of death: multiple blows to the head with a blunt instrument.

Other miscellaneous findings: (1) soap residue was discovered in the armpits and (2) the decedent had eaten a large meal about 1 hour prior to his death.

Daylight Saving Crime
Death was caused by a sharp wound to the abdomen, puncturing the small intestines and causing a massive loss of blood. The weapon was single-bladed with a serrated edge. Due to fire damage, the time of death cannot be established with any degree of accuracy.

Side note: The watch on the deceased's wrist was scorched but still functioning and only a minute off the correct time.

Gunfight at the O.K. Motel (Jackson Bosco)
Death was caused by a single 9-mm wound to the chest. The lack of abrasions on the wrists and ankles indicate that the deceased either made little effort, or was given little time, to try to loosen the sash cords tied to his hands and feet.

Gunfight at the O.K. Motel (Eugene "Buddy" Brinker)
Eighteen 9-mm bullets were recovered from the head and shoulder area, six potentially fatal. One 9-mm wound in central abdomen, also potentially fatal. From the amount and location of blood on the deceased's clothing, it can be deduced that the abdomen wound occurred first.

Manny, Moe, or Jack
Cause of death was a .38-caliber slug. It entered the chest, pierced the left auricle, and continued through the body, encountering no major bones. An exit wound exists ¾ inch below the left scapula. No bullet recovered. Powder burns on shirt indicate the gun had been held to the chest at the time of firing. Paraffin test was negative, however. The deceased had not fired a gun in the recent past.

A small contusion in the right rear parietal region indicates that the deceased had been hit over the head. The discoloration suggests that this occurred prior to death.

The Phantom Intruder
A .22-caliber bullet was recovered from the left hemisphere. Powder burns on the entry point (right temple) indicate it had been fired from point-blank range. No abrasions, contusions, or other signs of a struggle. Further examination of the brain reveals a sizable tumor. Malignant and probably inoperable.

Nonmedical note: The alarm on the deceased's wristwatch is set for 1:55 A.M.

Psychic Suicide
Death was caused by ingestion of potassium cyanide. Time of death can be established only loosely, anywhere from 1 hour to 1 minute before the body was discovered. There is a small, round burn mark on the back of the deceased's right hand. The lack of severe discoloration indicates that the burn occurred after death.

Shot in the Cul-de-Sac
Wendy Peterson, assistant medical examiner, presiding: .28-caliber slug removed from spinal area. The bullet split the third and fourth vertebrae and lodged in the lungs. A messy removal. Death probably occurred within seconds. Evidence bagged and sent to ballistics.

Paraffin test requested—results negative. The deceased had not fired a gun within the recent past.

The Show Girl Murders
Death was the result of a laceration to the right carotid artery. Angle and depth are consistent with a wound caused by flying glass. The presence of contusions on arms and legs suggests a fight or struggle. Pieces of skin under her fingernails indicate that the deceased scratched her assailant, probably leaving scratches or wounds of some kind.

Swallowing the Gun
No undigested food found in stomach. No trace of tranquilizers, depressants, or other sleep-inducing substances found in

stomach or blood analysis. Urine normal. No organ damage.

Minutes traces of phenothiazine, an insecticide, found in blood samples. Not nearly enough to be toxic.

Video Violence (Renaldo Jones)
A huge amount of blood had soaked through the deceased's left trouser leg. The bullet entered just above the knee, severing an artery and causing massive bleeding. A single bullet was retrieved from the leg. No other wounds are visible.

☞ Crime Scene Reports

Accidents Will Happen
The point of impact was on the passenger side, although the force had been enough to crush the grill, the hood, and the rest of the front. The entire windshield was shattered. Blood was splattered throughout the front and smeared on the driver's side air bag. It was found to be the same as the deceased's, O negative. In addition, the makeup mirror was in the down position. Both of the deceased's 3-inch high-heeled shoes were recovered from the front floor.

The Bearded Lady
The body's position and the bullet's trajectory indicate that Dr. Denton had been seated at his desk while his assailant stood across from him, perhaps at some distance.

On the floor by the door was a crumpled note that read: "I know what you're up to. If you want your secret to remain secret, come tonight. We'll discuss terms." The paper was unsigned, but the handwriting matched samples of Dr. Denton's.

Checking Out
Observing that a fire had recently burned in the fireplace, the police sifted the ashes and discovered 10 small white buttons and a tiny metallic hook-and-eye set. No prints were found on

the telephone. On comparing it to the size and shape of the wounds, the forensic squad was able to eliminate it as the murder weapon.

Daylight Saving Crime
Investigation by the arson unit has determined that the fire was the naturally occurring result of a lightning strike.

The corpse had been found underneath the floorboards of the burning structure, which saved it from further destruction. Also discovered on the scene were the charred remains of foodstuffs, miscellaneous supplies, a mattress, and a bread knife, presumed to be the murder weapon.

The Flighty Freshman
When the Myers' dormitory room was dusted, only two different sets of prints were found, one matching the deceased's, the other matching the prints lifted from Perry Winkler's confession. The murder weapon, an empty tequila bottle, had been wiped clean.

According to the victim's brother, no personal effects, other than Donovan's suitcase, are missing from the room.

Gunfight at the O.K. Motel
Four weapons were recovered from the room. A hunting knife with "Buddy" carved in the handle. Two semiautomatic .38-caliber rifles, one with a full clip, the other with twenty-one rounds fired. Twenty-one shell casings found on floor by window. Six full .38 clips found on the bed. One 9-mm handgun, five rounds in the clip along with one empty casing. No other 9-mm rounds or clips on site.

Blood samples were recovered from three locations on the carpet, behind the bed, by the window, and just inside the door.

How the Other Half Dies
The body had floated up near a little-used pier at the rear of the tannery grounds. The deceased was dressed in a beige evening dress, the clothing still mostly intact. A rope was found

tied around her waist, the end of it partly frayed and partly cut clean. Police divers entered the river and discovered the other end of the rope. It was tied around a large rock and was located directly under a wastewater drainage pipe from the facility. Divers took water samples to test for pollutants.

Last of the Royal Blood
When Ali discovered the body, it was warm to the touch, the blood around the wound still quite liquid. The shah was in pajamas and a robe. There was no sign of forced entry or of a struggle. A lamp beside the shah's reading chair was turned on. A book lay open on the end table beside a cup of warm mint tea.

Manny, Moe, or Jack
Several fragments of singed and bloody feathers are stuck to the inside of the deceased's shirt near the bullet's entry point. Beneath the shattered window only three tiny shards of glass are found lying on the floor. At the foot of the bed is a copper cuspidor, a large dent in its side. The key to the room lies on the oak floor, just inside the bedroom door. As for the .38 on the bed, it was the property of the deceased and, according to the housekeeper, was normally kept in his desk.

Finally, according to the housekeeper, a piece of furniture has been moved. The bureau that had been against the wall facing the bed is now against the wall next to the French windows.

Psychic Suicide
The room's only window is locked from the inside. The door is equipped with a simple thumb lock on the knob. A book of matches is on the table along with one used match, the cup, and the incense candle. The room is outfitted with a single bed, hot plate, two cupboards, two end tables, a dining table, file cabinet, two chairs, a television, a clock radio, and a motorized wheelchair. No other electronic or battery-powered devices. Contents of closet, cupboards, and bathroom have not

been listed. The key to the file cabinet was found in the deceased's shirt pocket.

Shot in the Cul-de-Sac (Abe Leary, Homicide Squad, 5:18 P.M.)
Kitchen: The coffeemaker is on. One cigarette is stubbed out in ashtray. A coffee cup is on floor by door, broken into four pieces. The footprints preserved on the wet floor have been compromised. One print, matching the deceased's slipper, is still discernible. Other set was accidentally obliterated by the assistant medical examiner when she walked through. A .22 slug recovered from doorjamb (bagged for evidence).

Living Room: One lamp knocked over. Blood on area rug in middle of room (sample bagged for evidence). No weapon. Two different sets of fingerprints recovered.

A later examination matched the prints to the deceased and his spouse.

The Show Girl Murders (Dolly's Dressing Room)
The disheveled state of the dressing room points to a struggle having taken place. A pair of severely torn and bloodied elbow-length gloves lies on the floor. The rest of the deceased's costume is hanging neatly in the closet. The only clear prints lifted from the room match those of the three show girls who shared the dressing room.

Swallowing the Gun
Wastebasket contains two pieces of unopened junk mail.

Joke-a-Day desk calendar reveals the date, May 13. Handwritten on the page is the following: "Lunch—Milton—1. Meet here."

Victim's prints are recovered from the safe, the corporation files, and the gun barrel. Partial print of victim's right forefinger lifted from trigger.

Video Violence
The weapon, an unregistered Smith & Wesson .38, was found 40 feet to the right of Renaldo's body. A cloth, used to wipe it clean of prints, was found tied around the handle. Two spent shell casings were in the chamber. A third casing, from the same gun, was found in a ravine halfway between the house and the murder site. The police have determined that the body was located a brisk 5-minute walk from his house. The farmer's house is a brisk 10-minute walk in the opposite direction.

✐ Lab & Hospital Reports

Accidents Will Happen (Paul Adidas)
Patient was admitted to the emergency room at 10:17 P.M. with a stomach puncture, two broken ribs, and multiple bruises to the chest, as well as a hairline fracture of the left shoulder.

The attending physician was impressed by the unusually symmetrical nature of the injuries. When asked if the wounds could possibly be self-inflicted, he replies, "No way. From their position and severity, I'd say impossible. And Mr. Adidas could have died if he hadn't been brought in when he was."

The Bearded Lady (Poison Analysis)
A stool sample taken from Amelia Perdue by Dr. Denton revealed traces of salmonella, a bacterial poison associated with contaminated egg or meat products. Salmonella symptoms vary in intensity and usually occur 24 to 36 hours after infection.

How the Other Half Dies (Test Water Sample)
An analysis of the water in the area of the drainage pipe revealed large concentrations of tannic acid, dihydroxyacetone, and other agents used in the processing and preservation of

leather. These amounts exceed acceptable levels outlined by the federal government. Laboratory results have been turned over to the Environmental Protection Agency for disciplinary action.

Shot in the Cul-de-Sac (Ballistics Test)
The rifling marks on the .28 shell removed from the deceased match the marks produced by the weapon recovered from the woods. The handgun in question is registered in the name of the deceased's wife, Marlene Smucker. A partial latent print on the inside of the handle is a match of the print from Mrs. Smucker's right ring finger.

 Miscellaneous Examinations

The Bearded Lady (Desktop)
Among the stamps located on the desk within easy reach of the victim were an 1862 Franklin 1 cent, an 1870 Washington 5 cent, and the previously mentioned 1870 Queen Victoria black penny, defaced with a moustache and beard. Also on the desk were various mounts, adhesives, labels, and a magnifier.

The Flighty Freshman (Holographic Results)
Perry's test papers are examined by a handwriting expert. While some of the samples match the writing found in the confession, other samples do not. "They are all similar," he testifies. "But some are definitely the work of a second person. From the belabored and uneven nature of the script, I would also hypothesize that both people were right-handed but had, for whatever reason, written with their lefts."

One of Perry's acquaintances recalled that he seemed to be left-handed.

Last of the Royal Blood (Guests' Luggage)
Chuck's luggage: In addition to usual clothing was the *Book of Mormon*, and *Murder Impossible*, an anthology of mystery stories.

Rodney's luggage: In addition to usual, one diamond stud earring, driver's license showing Rodney with a moustache, the latest issue of *PC Magazine*, and the book *A Cultural History of Ibabi*.

Mary Ann's luggage: In addition to usual, one large, gold hoop earring, and paisley blouse, same pattern as her gift wrapping. No reading matter.

The Show Girl Murders (Broken Mirror)
A large fire extinguisher stationed beside the hall mirror had been used to shatter it. Probably thrown. No latent fingerprints found on either fire extinguisher or on glass fragments.

Video Violence (Gregory's Video)
On the video: Renaldo is speaking to the camera when he sees something and stops, frightened. A shot rings out. The television host screams, grabbing his lower left leg. Turning now, the camera fixes on a masked figure standing by a rock and dressed in camouflage fatigues. It is wearing gloves and pointing a gun. The figure hesitates, as if confused or indecisive, then turns and runs off.

The camera returns to Renaldo holding his leg. A small patch of blood oozes through his fingers. The camera is switched off.

☛ Miscellaneous Searches

Accidents Will Happen (Area near Crash Site)
A half mile from the crash site, on a road running perpendicular to it, the police inspect a public phone booth and discover traces of human blood on the receiver, coin slot, and rotary dial. It is analyzed and found to match the victim's type, O negative. Three cigarette butts, one also bearing a blood smear, are found on the ground nearby.

Phone company records show a call having been made from here to the Boitano Cement Co. at 8:21 A.M., approximately 10 minutes after the crash.

The Bearded Lady (Livery Mansion)
A thorough search of the Livery mansion failed to shed any light on the murder or on a possible motive. A used disposable razor was retrieved from the kitchen wastebasket and another from the library wastebasket. Although not commonly found in such locations, the two razors do not seem germane to the investigation.

Checking Out (Murder Weapon)
Pearl Lowe was a sales representative for the Edison Pipe Co. Her sample case was found lying open on the floor beside the table. The police noted that a sample was missing. Two officers were assigned to wade through the hotel garbage and recovered a 12-inch length of steel alloy pipe. It had been wiped clean, but microscopic examination revealed traces of blood plus fragments of skin and bone.

Checking Out (Hotel Closet)
In the closet used by Bob Williams were the following: two business suits, tuxedo jacket and pants, two neckties, one white shirt, one tuxedo shirt, set of studs and cuff links, cummerbund,

two pairs of black shoes, one pair of loafers, two polo shirts, pair of chino slacks, two pressed T-shirts, and a sweater.

Daylight Saving Crime (Coast near Beach House)
A jet ski was discovered washed up on the beach a quarter mile from Phil Okan's house. The make, model, and serial numbers match those of a jet ski purchased by the deceased 2 months ago, paid for with a credit card. The seat was adjusted to its lowest position, as were the handlebars.

Gunfight at the O.K. Motel (Jack's Car)
Glove compartment: A box of 9-mm shells.

Trunk: Suitcase containing personal possessions. Sample case containing ladies' lingerie. Two bank bags, each containing a quarter of a million in $100 bills.

Last of the Royal Blood (Mud Room)
A utility room often found at the rear of New England homes, a mud room is used for storage of coats and outdoor gear and as an informal entrance. A search of this mud room produced these items: four pairs of skis and ski poles, four pairs of ski boots, sizes 9 to 11. Four pairs of snowshoes, sizes 9 to 11. Assorted coats, hats, scarves, heavy socks, and gloves, including those of all three guests. Five pairs of ice skates, sizes 6, 9, 9½, 10, 11.

Last of the Royal Blood (Grand Hall)
On the wall beside the grand hall fireplace, an ornamental dagger is missing from an arrangement of traditional weapons. On the top surface of a tile display shelf, beside a row of Ibabi carvings, Ali notices a patch of rust about 5 inches square.

Manny, Moe, or Jack (Bedroom Fireplace)
Among the fireplace ashes were found the following charred remains: (1) a small fabric remnant, heavy cotton, color undetermined, (2) various feather remnants, type undetermined, and (3) shell casing from a .38-caliber bullet.

Manny, Moe, or Jack (Outside Bedroom Window)
Numerous glass fragments were found on the balcony outside
the French windows. An inspection of the maple tree located
30 feet from the window resulted in the discovery of a .38-
caliber slug lodged in the bark. Initial theory holds that this
bullet passed through the deceased, broke the window, and still
had the power to imbed itself in the tree. The apparent lack
of rifling marks on the bullet, however, may serve to discredit
this theory.

Manny, Moe, or Jack (Behind Bedroom Bureau)
The bedroom bureau was moved from its position beside the
French windows. Nothing was found behind it or on the floor.
There exists, however, a slight, round indentation in the wall,
approximately 3 feet off the floor. It is less than 1 inch in di-
ameter and less than ½ inch deep. The inside is curved and
comes to a point in the center.

The Phantom Intruder (Woods)
A .22-caliber handgun was found ⅓ mile behind the restaurant
and has been identified as the weapon. An accumulation of mud
and debris makes it impossible to dust for prints. A short length
of twine is tied around the gun handle. The end of the twine
appears to have been torn off.
    In a shallow pit just inches from the gun, a cache of 13 buried
bones was also found. Identified as animal bones, predomi-
nantly cow and pig.

The Phantom Intruder (Teddy and Esther's Bedroom)
A bundle of love letters is discovered hidden under the edge
of the carpet in Esther Gouda's closet. All are addressed to
Esther Gouda in care of a post office box and signed, "your
loving Paul." The earliest letters are dated 6 months ago.

Psychic Suicide (Behind House)
The victim's room is on the ground floor. Its only window
faces onto a small, sunny backyard, sheltered on three sides by

a wooden fence. Access to the yard can be gained from the kitchen door or around the side of the house. In the center is a solitary oak tree. Hanging from a branch is a crystal wind chime. The central crystal is about 5 inches across and double-convex in shape. The landlady testifies that the ornament first appeared on the tree sometime last week. She assumed it had been placed there by one of her boarders.

Shot in the Cul-de-Sac (Bedroom)
A box of .28 shells was found in a bedside drawer. No prints on the drawer knob or on the box. Gun oil on drawer lining indicates a handgun had been stored here.

The bed linen is mussed. Two empty glasses of wine on end table. One glass bears prints matching the deceased's. Other glass has red lipstick marks on rim and no prints. Sheets and towels have been taken in for hair and fiber analysis.

Shot in the Cul-de-Sac (Woods)
A search of the woods with metal detectors produced a .28-caliber handgun. The weapon had been wiped clean. However, one latent print was recovered from the inside of the handle. The gun had been buried in a patch of brush just out of sight of the highway. Not far away, an officer noticed a fresh scar in the bark of a birch tree. Paraffin tests show that a bullet had been fired into the tree trunk from a distance of approximately 20 feet. No bullet was recovered from the soft wood.

Video Violence (Letter Hidden in Drawer)
"Dearest Jane,

I know we have to wait. Each moment away from you is torture. Sneaking around together in the shadows is a mere tease of the happiness I know we can give each other. I trust you about the divorce. I know it has to be handled right. Neither one of us wants to be poor. All the same, I can barely contain myself. If there's anything I can do to speed things along, let me know.

Your Adoring Slave" (unsigned)

🏠 Research

The Flighty Freshman (Perry's School Records)
Perry's college records indicate that he's not academically in-clined. Enrolled primarily in lecture hall courses, he has a spotty attendance record and barely maintains a C average.

Upon checking out Perry's transcripts, the police discover that his high school records are complete fakes. No one named Perry Winkler ever attended that high school. His parents did not live at the address given. In fact, no one in his alleged hometown has ever heard of him.

Gunfight at the O.K. Motel (Investigation of Jack's Past)
An inquiry into Jackson Bosco's past reveals a Colorado Springs, Colorado, arrest record dating from 3 years ago. He had two separate counts of drunk and disorderly, one count of assault, and one count of resisting arrest. All counts were dropped.

Further investigation reveals no prior contact between Bosco and the men suspected in the Planters' National Bank robbery.

How the Other Half Dies (Phone Records)
The telephone company has determined that no long-distance calls were put through to the Carlton beach house at any time on Saturday morning or afternoon. No records exist for local calls.

The Phantom Intruder (Experiment with Barking Dog)
Hershey is placed alone downstairs. One at a time, each suspect enters the house, then leaves. In most cases, the dog erupts into a violent fit of barking. He refrains only in the case of family members, Esther and Oscar Gouda.

Swallowing the Gun *(Medical Guide to Poisons)*
Phenothiazine (cont.), *p. 237:*
Symptoms: Contact with this substance in its liquid or gas state commonly results in irritation to the respiratory tract. In large amounts, it can cause liver and kidney damage. Large doses also result in falling blood pressure, darkened urine, impotence, and muscle damage. Convulsions and disturbances in cardiac rhythm have been known to occur, but not in every case.

$ Wills & Insurance

The Bearded Lady (Joshua Livery's Will)
Joshua Livery's most recent will was drawn up 3 months prior to his death. In it he leaves his entire estate to Amelia Perdue. In the event that Amelia Perdue is no longer alive, dies before the will is probated, or cannot be located within a 6-month period, the estate was to be divided equally between Benjamin and Victoria Livery.

Daylight Saving Crime (Richie's Estate)
Okan Brothers Hardware has declared bankruptcy. Both brothers filed suits against each other alleging financial irresponsibility and misappropriation of funds. On the Friday before Richie vanished, Linda Okan closed out the savings and checking accounts. Mrs. Okan remains the beneficiary of her husband's $1-million insurance policy.

The Phantom Intruder (Teddy Gouda's Will and Insurance)
Chef Teddy's lawyer testifies that a month ago his client dictated a new will and requested a change of beneficiary. In both cases, Esther Gouda's name was removed and replaced with Oscar Gouda's. Due to the violent nature of death, Mr. Gouda's insurance policy will pay double indemnity.

Analysis of Evidence

Accidents Will Happen

Several facts point to Lana having been a passenger at the time of the crash, i.e., the lowered mirror, her half-applied makeup, and the 3-inch high heels which would have made driving difficult. The broken right clavicle indicates that she'd been in the passenger seat with her shoulder harness secured. In addition, the blood smear on the air bag shows that she'd been moved into the driver's seat after the blood had been shed. The absence of a tire squeal reveals that the brakes had not been applied.

The pay phone call to Boitano proves nothing but does implicate the mobster. More important than the call are the cigarette butts. They say something significant about the crime. Also significant is the attack on Pauly and the resultant injuries.

The Bearded Lady

Dr. Denton faced his killer long enough to allow him to draw a beard on the stamp, a clue that was small and subtle enough to escape his killer's attention. A look at the other stamps, however, does little to illuminate his intent. If he'd meant to finger Ben Livery, then why didn't he grab the Franklin stamp or draw a goatee on that stamp? Likewise, to implicate Vicky or George Trent, he could have simply grabbed the Victoria or the Washington stamp. So, he must have been trying to communicate something else.

The presence of salmonella in Amelia's system shows that her poisoning was accidental and might have occurred before her arrival at the Livery house. The disposable razors are significant due to their location. Someone either used the razors in the kitchen and library or went out of his or her way to dispose of them in these public rooms.

Checking Out

The buttons and the tiny hook-and-eye found in the fireplace indicate that articles of clothing may have been burned there. This is supported by the fact that a dress shirt and a tuxedo bow tie seem to be missing from the closet.

A few other oddities stand out. Judging from the contents of his stomach, Williams had recently eaten. And yet he had just ordered dinner from room service. Also, why had the phone been pulled from the wall? True, this could have happened during a struggle, except that there's no real evidence of a struggle. The deathbed clue doesn't make sense either, leading to a supposition that the ring and pearl were purposely planted by the killer in order to mislead the police.

One mystery that's easily solved, the naked corpse. The soap residue shows that Williams may have been in the middle of a shower at the time he confronted his attacker.

Daylight Saving Crime

Richie Okan did not die on the island. Several facts point to this: the absence of blood on Palmetto Island, the presence of the knife in the shack, and most significant, the fact that Richie's watch had been reset from daylight saving time to standard time, something that wouldn't have occurred if he'd been killed Saturday morning. It was Richie who was holed up in the shack and who visited the store that night. Given these facts, it also seems clear that Linda and Richie set up Phil for the faked murder, probably to gain the insurance money and start a new life far away from their old debts.

The only question remaining is, who really killed Richie and how?

The Flighty Freshman

The crime scene provides a pair of peculiarities: (1) Only two people's prints were found. Logically, three sets should have been in the room. (2) Although a suitcase was taken from the Myers's dorm room, nothing else seems to be missing, and none of their possessions were found in Perry's apartment.

From the handwriting evidence, it appears as though someone had been occasionally masquerading as Perry or at least taking some of his tests. The captain was struck by the fact that both writers had attempted to disguise their penmanship.

But what most intrigued Captain Mallory was Danny Myers's alibi. Why would an apparently inebriated senior go out to study on a Saturday night? And with the same girl whom his brother had been dating?

Gunfight at the O.K. Motel

To get a handle on the case, we have to pay attention to the guns. Both men were killed with 9-mm bullets. This rules out the .38 semiautomatics in the robbers' possession. It rules in the police assault weapons and the 9-mm handgun. The weird thing about the handgun is that no extra rounds were found in the room, even though the robbers were well supplied with other ammo. A box of 9-mm shells was found in Jack's car; so, we may speculate that the handgun belonged to Jack.

Since only his head and shoulders were visible above the windowsill, it seems improbable that Buddy would be hit in the stomach by a police bullet. The blood stain by the door also seems odd.

Given this evidence, the money in Jack's car, and his violent, impulsive history, he can no longer be considered just an unlucky hostage.

How the Other Half Dies

There is some disagreement about what Tracy wore on the night she vanished. The maid described it as beige while the waitress clearly recalled it as brown with a hat. Over an hour passed between the time they left the penthouse and arrived at the restaurant. Something could have happened to require a change of clothes.

Tracy's body had been weighed down with a rock, presumably in order to keep the body from being discovered. And yet the rope tying her to the rock had been partly severed. This indicates that the killer wanted the body discovered, just not right away.

The phone records allow only two possibilities. Either Bryce lied about Tracy's call to him on Saturday, or Tracy made the call locally.

The presence of polluting chemicals in the water were not taken into account when the preliminary autopsy was performed. A more complete autopsy seems required.

Last of the Royal Blood

None of the guests knew the shah or were related to him; so, the only possible motive is political assassination. Since the assassin probably didn't want to hang around, we can assume that Ali's discovery of the body so soon after the murder interrupted the assassin's flight plans. Escape routes would be limited. The lack of snow precluded skiing to safety while the guards, dogs, and fences would discourage most land-based escape.

The guest luggage gave Ali some food for thought. The solo hoop earring seems like an odd thing for Mary Ann to pack. And a comparison of their reading material, while revealing nothing about motive, might shed some light on the killer's plans.

The clues from the grand hall both seem significant. The missing dagger must undoubtedly be the murder weapon. And the small, rusty square on the tile shelf shows that a metal object had been standing there but was now missing.

Manny, Moe, or Jack

Rifling marks are the distinctive markings left on a bullet by a gun barrel. It's the primary way in which ballistics experts match a bullet to a specific gun. The absence of rifling marks on a spent shell is extremely rare.

The existence of feather remnants inside the shirt suggest that the killer placed a pillow between shirt and chest, probably to muffle the gunshot. The pillow was then burned in the fireplace. The glass fragments on the balcony indicate that the shot that broke the window came from inside. The bureau was probably moved in an attempt to hide the indentation in the wall which resembles the mark made by a low-impact bullet, a bullet, for instance, that had just gone all the way through a body. From this and other evidence, it's logical to assume that there were two shots—one that the killer wanted to keep quiet and one that he wanted to be heard.

The Phantom Intruder
The fact that Teddy had set his watch alarm for 1:55 A.M. indicates that he lied about hearing a burglar and that Paul was telling the truth about their 2 A.M. appointment. The mud on the gun, the twine around the handle, and the proximity of buried bones all point to a four-footed accomplice who may have carried the weapon away from the scene. The figure in the woods and the swinging French doors might also be the result of Hershey's involvement.

The tumor and the change in the will, although important to Teddy, would be important to the others only if they knew about them. And there's no evidence that Teddy shared either piece of information.

Psychic Suicide
The appearance of the wind chime just a week before the murder is highly suspect. Also, the postmortem burn mark on the victim's hand deserves serious thought. How could it have gotten there?

If Noah is telling the truth, and we don't know that he is, then someone called him and rescheduled his session with the swami. The most sensible conclusion is that it was the killer. He or she needed this particular hour alone with the victim in order to carry out or cover up the murder.

The object missing from the victim's room? Think about it. A paraplegic with a clock radio and television, but no battery-powered device? What about the television's remote control? A remote control would be essential and yet none was found.

Shot in the Cul-de-Sac

The physical evidence recovered in this case is among the most confusing we've ever encountered. This, in itself, should be a clue.

First the simple stuff. A bathrobe after 4 P.M.? Wine glasses and lipstick? It's clear, Ed had recently engaged in sex. Even though the coffee cup and cigarette in the kitchen suggest that his bed partner had left before Ed met his death, this still has the look of a crime of passion.

We have evidence of two guns, a .22 and a .28. We know that Ed himself didn't fire a gun and yet the single obliterated set of footprints suggests a single killer. Was the killer wielding two guns, then? Highly unlikely.

The officer arrived at the house only minutes after the shots. Yet no car was seen leaving the area and no intruder was seen running across the lawns. The killer's timetable was very tight. Yet various prints upstairs and down had been wiped away. When could this have been done?

The shot in the night, the buried gun, and the injured tree seem to make no sense. Why would someone draw attention to the woods and then bury a gun there, right by the highway? The only explanation is a frame-up attempt. Someone is trying to arrange the evidence to frame Marlene Smucker.

The Show Girl Murders

The bulk of evidence points to an unpremeditated attack, perhaps the result of a fight. The assailant may be hiding one or more wounds.

Tim seems to have been caught in a contradiction. In his first statement, he claimed to have seen Deedee and Dora standing by the fire extinguisher in the side hall. In his second statement, he denies ever having seen the full-length mirror, beside the extinguisher and directly in his line of sight.

In lieu of other possible motives, the one expressed by Johnny the doorman deserves consideration.

Swallowing The Gun

Since the victim's prints are on the safe and the folder, it's reasonable to assume that Hank had been curious enough about Barlow's theory to fetch the pertinent documents and look them over. And since today's page has been torn off the calendar and is not found in the wastebasket, it's also reasonable to assume that the killer had lunch scheduled with the deceased today and removed the page containing a note of this appointment.

Next comes the autopsy report. The traces of insecticide were minimal, but the old lieutenant did his homework nonetheless. He discovered that the only symptom Hank might have suffered from after his exposure to the insecticide was a sore throat. A sore throat? Hmm.

Video Violence

The autopsy places the wound on Renaldo's upper leg. But Gregory's video shows Renaldo grabbing his leg below the knee. The autopsy also mentions massive bleeding, something not seen in the video. The bullet casing found in the woods tells us that a third shot was fired from the murder weapon, but we don't know when or where.

Both Gregory and Fred have alibis. Gregory wouldn't have had time to return to the house and shoot Jane. Fred was on the phone during this period, and his phone partner swears she heard the gunshot while on the line with Fred.

The unset alarm points to an inside job. The slight discrepancy in the killer's physical description points to the possibility of two people using the same costume.

The love letters are illuminating, but two more puzzles confront us. Why was the gun so near Renaldo's body? And why did the killer discard the costume in the shed?

Accidents Will Happen—Solution
(1) His injuries came from the car accident, not a mob attack. (2) Pauly Adidas. (3) The driver, Pauly, used the car's one air bag to save his own life.

Lana's fatal mistake was not realizing that her boyfriend might also be a crime-family member. After the Salvatore divorce, Tony Boitano enlisted his handsomest young soldier to woo the divorcée to keep her under control. All the while Agent Cullen was trying to get Lana to testify, Pauly was doing his best to talk her out of it.

On the morning of the crash, Pauly's car was in the shop. He was in the process of driving Lana to work when she made her fateful call. Pauly was in a bind. He had to silence Lana before they arrived at FBI headquarters without exposing himself. An obvious murder would throw too much heat on the family. It had to be an accident.

Both Lana and Pauly were wearing seat belts. But only the driver's side was equipped with an air bag. Pauly trusted this, and with a flip of the wheel, he sent the car off the road, down into the ravine.

Lana wasn't quite dead, not yet, but Pauly didn't want to do anything that might jeopardize the "accidental" evidence. He dragged her over to the driver's side, completed the job of smashing the windshield, then hobbled off. Pauly had noticed a pay phone along the road shortly before the crash. Now he walked through the woods and put in a call to Boitano. The three cigarette butts showed that someone had been waiting there, probably waiting for a ride. When the police saw this, they knew the crime had been unpremeditated and that no second car was involved.

The air bag saved Pauly's life, but he desperately needed medical attention. Going to a doctor, even a discreet "family" doctor, would have resulted in bed time, bandages, and possible suspicion. So, Pauly faked the attack on himself to account for his injuries.

The cigarette butts got Agent Cullen focused in the right direction, but it was a 25-cent piece that sealed the case. When he opened the phone's cash box, Cullen discovered a blood-stained quarter. Perfectly preserved on one side of it was Pauly's right thumbprint.

The Bearded Lady—Solution

(1) Amelia (aka Alex) Perdue.   (2) He had discovered her secret.   (3) Denton was saying his killer was a man disguised as a woman.

A simple clue, contained in the story itself, holds the mystery's key. When Amelia gulped and her choker bobbed, it showed that an Adam's apple was hidden underneath. Amelia was a man.

As the first rumors stated, the real Amelia died years ago. However, her twin brother Alex was very much alive, and when he heard that a law firm was looking for his sister, he secretly learned that his sister was an heiress and if she were dead, the fortune would revert to Joshua's relatives. Alex already possessed his sister's old documents. All he had to do now was to play Amelia for a few weeks, until the estate was settled.

The disguise was going well. He used thick makeup and shaved twice a day, always carefully disposing of the razors. But then, he had an unfortunate attack of food poisoning. While Alex was unconscious, Dr. Denton examined him, discovered his secret, and decided to blackmail him in return for a share of the fortune.

Alex sneaked over to the doctor's house and confronted him. Denton was working on his stamps, his pen in hand. But he couldn't just write down the name of his attacker. Alex would see it and remove it. So, he did the next best thing—drawing a beard on a woman's face, trying to reveal that what seemed like an old woman was really an old man.

Checking Out—Solution

(1) Scotty, the waiter.   (2) A botched robbery.   (3) Scotty planted the clue, assuming Pearl was Bob's wife.

The police started off on the wrong foot by assuming that robbery wasn't the motive. It was. Shortly after 3 P.M. Scotty knocked on the door. When no one answered, he used his pass key. This was his modus operandi, robbing the rooms when the guests were out.

Williams heard a noise and emerged naked from the shower. Scotty tried to fast-talk his way out, but Williams wasn't buying. Murder seemed the only way out. During Scotty's attack, blood spattered on his uniform. This created a problem. How could he go back to work with a bloody shirt and bow tie? Scotty solved his problem by burning them both, then stealing a shirt and tie, a black tie, from the closet.

He didn't take any valuables, hoping this would mislead the police. Then he got a brainstorm. By dragging the body to the dresser and planting the ring and tie tack, he could pin the blame on Williams's wife, Pearl. Like the rest of the staff, Scotty assumed they were married. As part of the same plan, he tore the phone from the wall. If Williams had been able to use a phone, then such a convoluted deathbed clue would have looked suspicious.

As for the steak dinner, Scotty didn't want to leave the discovery of the body to chance. He himself placed the room service order, right before tearing out the phone.

Scotty's plan might have worked but was foiled by a fellow employee. Sam, a part-time waiter, wanted Scotty's job. He reported Scotty to management for wearing a black tie instead of the regulation brown tie issued to all Chantel employees. The police heard about this and it set them on the right track.

Daylight Saving Crime—Solution

(1) Rev. Cal Brown with Linda as an accomplice.   (2) For love and the insurance money.   (3) Richie was faking death, but Cal made it real.

Phil and Linda were not lovers. And that calls into question the Rev. Brown's story. After all, he was the one who told the police this and requested the investigation.

Richie and Linda had been planning his "death" for some time and their animosity toward Phil made him the perfect patsy. They dropped Richie's ring and buckle into the picnic firepit, then shoveled dirt and ashes over them. Richie, who was dropped off at a deserted pier, sneaked into the abandoned shack, planning to stay put until the search for his body died down. Once the trial was over, Linda would join him someplace where they could start a new life.

Linda, however, preferred to start her new life with a new husband. She and the Rev. Cal were the real lovers. While police attention was focused on Phil, Cal visited the shack, killing Richie with the bread knife and stuffing his body under the floorboards, where it might never be discovered.

To further incriminate Phil, Cal took out the jet ski and ditched it in the water not far from Phil's beach house. This proved to be his undoing. The police noticed that the seat and handlebars were adjusted for a short person. The Okan men were both large, a fact that set the police looking for someone of smaller stature.

The Flighty Freshman — Solution

(1) Perry never existed; he was a joke concocted by the Myers brothers. (2) His brother Danny. (3) Crime of passion—a drunken fight over a girl.

Perry Winkler never existed. The school pranksters, Donovan and Danny, had invented the mythical student just to see if they could pull it off. The brothers took turns donning the wig and other bits of disguise to become Perry. They occasionally showed up for Perry's lecture hall classes and alternated taking his exams, always using their left hands in order to change the handwriting.

Donovan had just returned to the dorm dressed as Perry. Danny, drunk and belligerent, ran into him in the hall. But instead of leaving, Danny followed his brother back into their room. They cranked up the stereo and began to argue about Alicia. This much of "Perry's" confession was true. Donovan had been killed in a drunken fight over a girl.

Danny thought that the only way to escape a murder charge was to frame the nonexistent Perry. He packed up the few pieces of Perry's accessories they kept in their room and fled, wearing the disguise. Arriving at Perry's apartment, Danny wrote out the confession, then ran over to Alicia's and told her everything. Alicia was devastated, but she still cared for Danny. She knew it had been an accident and wasn't about to turn him over to the police. She gave him the alibi he needed. Danny's story fell apart when the police matched his prints with those found on Perry's confession.

Gunfight at the O.K. Motel—Solution

(1) Jack killed Buddy, planning to steal the already stolen money. (2) The police interrupted Jack's getaway. (3) He was killed by a stray police bullet.

If we begin with the assumption that our impulsive, violent Jack Bosco recognized the robbers from the television news, then the rest falls into place. Instead of driving off, Jack watched the bandits sneak the million dollars into their room. He watched and thought. And when one of the robbers left to go shopping, Jack made his move.

With the handgun from his glove compartment, Jack knocked on the motel door, pretending to be the manager. He made short work of the solo robber, shooting him in the stomach. Jack transferred the first two bags of money to his trunk and was about to exit with bags three and four when the patrol car pulled up.

What to do? Jack couldn't leave. Could he bluff his way out as a good citizen who struggled with a criminal and had shot him in self-defense? Well, not with all that money in his trunk.

Jack did the only think he could think of, propping Buddy Brinker's body up in a chair, starting the gunfight, then tying himself up, and hobbling for the safety of the bathroom. It was a risky move, but then he could explain that they were planning to take his car and use him as a hostage. No one would be the wiser. He'd even be a media hero. The only thing Jack didn't take into consideration was the stray police bullet catching him on the way.

How the Other Half Dies — Solution

(1) In the river; she was killed Friday night.   (2) Bryce with Anna as an accomplice.   (3) Anna masqueraded as Tracy at the restaurant.

The motive was only hinted at. Bryce was Tracy's guardian, responsible for her money until she turned 21. But Bryce had long ago embezzled his sister's inheritance. As her heir, he realized that murder would be the only way to cover up his crime.

Bryce wanted Tracy to wear her favorite brown dress and hat. That's because Anna had already purchased a copy of them. On their way to the restaurant, Bryce made a detour, using his keys to gain entry to the tannery through a little-used gate. Once at the pier, he shot Tracy, weighted her body down and dumped it by the drainage pipe. As a tannery owner, Bryce knew about the preserving properties of his waste water. By the time the rope broke and she bobbed to the surface, the chemicals would have sufficiently confused the time of death and given him an alibi.

Anna, who was about the same size and build as Tracy, was waiting outside the gates, disguised in the brown dress and concealing hat. They went to a new restaurant where no one knew them. Anna caused a scene and made sure she exited before any of their friends arrived. While Anna changed and drove out to the beach house, Bryce stayed in the public arena, giving himself an alibi throughout the weekend.

On Saturday, Anna shopped for groceries for their guests and used the opportunity to make a phony call to the house, preserving the illusion that Tracy was still alive.

This mystery is based on an actual New Jersey murder in which a polluted river confused autopsy results just enough to give the killer an alibi. In that case, as in this one, the mistake was eventually realized and the culprit brought to justice.

Last of the Royal Blood—Solution

(1) "Mary Ann." (2) Hired by the Ibabi government. (3) By skating across the frozen lake.

At the time our story opened, the real Mary Ann Nilson lay dead in her Atlanta home, the victim of an assassin hired by Ibabi to kill the last member of the royal family. Shannon Gibbs had been trying to gain access to the shah for some time. When Rodney began bragging over the Internet about his upcoming visit, Shannon knew this was her chance. She wheedled her way into Mary Ann's apartment, killed the unwitting woman, and took her place.

Shannon had done research on the shah but was unprepared for his birthday celebration. Finding herself without a present, she faked her way brilliantly, taking one of the hundreds of knickknacks from the hall, wrapping it in a scarf, fastening it with an earring loop, and presenting the birthday boy with a statute he already owned. Soon enough someone would discover her trick, but by then the shah would be dead and she would be gone.

Her escape plan was just as clever. Before dinner, Shannon took a pair of ice skates (women's size 6) from her luggage and planted them in the mud room. Right after the murder, she would sneak downstairs, slip on her blades, and skate across the frozen lake to a spot where a car was waiting.

Shannon had just finished tying up her skates when the alarm sounded and the doors automatically locked. She had no choice but to remove them, race into the nearby kitchen, and pretend to be making a midnight sandwich. She would try to brazen it out.

Ali grew suspicious when he noticed that "Mary Ann" had been the only guest to arrive without a book or magazine. She obviously didn't intend to be there long enough to do any reading. But before Ali could fit the pieces together, the police arrived and took all three suspects into custody. The real Mary Ann Nilson's body was discovered the very next morning.

Manny, Moe, or Jack—Solution

(1) Adolph's middle son, Moe.   (2) He quietly shot him, then placed a bullet in the fire to explode later.

Before visiting his father's room, Moe took wet wood and set up crackling fires in all six downstairs fireplaces. Once in Adolph's room, Moe hit his unsuspecting father over the head with the cuspidor. Then he sat the unconscious man up on the bed, placed a throw pillow under Adolph's shirt, and shot him in the heart. The pillow, the crackling fires, and the fact that the gun was a pistol, not a revolver, all helped muffle the shot.

Unexpectedly, however, the bullet went straight through the old man, denting the wall. Moe retrieved the bullet then moved the bureau to cover up the dent.

His next step was to burn the pillow, then place his father's prints on the gun. Just before leaving the room, Moe threw a .38 cartridge into the fire. In a few minutes, when he was safely downstairs with an alibi, the bullet would explode from the heat. He had no way of knowing where the shell would end up. That he left to chance. After locking the door behind him, Moe slid the key back underneath, then went down to join Manny. When the bullet did explode, it shot across the room, through the pane of glass and into a nearby tree, thereby implicating Jack, for a short time at least.

If Moe had had time to retrieve the casing from the grate, his plan might have succeeded. But the police were immediately drawn by the smell of the burned pillow. Once the feathers and casing were found, the solution was obvious. Whichever son had last visited Adolph must be his killer.

Phantom Intruder — Solution

(1) Chef Teddy killed himself.   (2) Teddy used his dog to get rid of the weapon.   (3) It was tied to a meat bone; Hershey tried to bury it.

No wonder Teddy was depressed. His wife and partner were having an affair, and he was dying of a brain tumor. The last few months of his life did not present a very cheery prospect. Suicide would end the pain, give his father a decent amount of money, and, if he worked it right, get his partner convicted of murder.

Teddy began taking his chocolate labrador out into the woods and training him not to be spooked by gunshots. This accomplished, he called up Paul, arranging for him to be on the scene of the "crime" at just the right moment.

On the night of his suicide, Teddy awoke just before 2 A.M., alerted both witnesses, then retrieved his dog and gun. Down in the rear dining room, he unlatched the French doors, improvised a one-sided conversation, then shot himself in the head. At first the smell of blood unnerved the dog. But Hershey hadn't been fed all day and instinct soon took over. The gun, lying in Teddy's hand, was tied to a meaty ham bone. Hershey grabbed the bone and raced out the doors, setting them swinging. After years of handing out soup bones, Teddy knew Hershey's habit and was confident that the gun would soon join the bones in the dog's secret hole.

With the discovery of the gun and Paul's alibi, Teddy's plot began to unravel. Why would he call out Paul Esterbrook's name? Why would he set his alarm for 1:55 A.M., then lie about the burglar? And why had he spent so much time with Hershey in the woods? The answer was clear, but the sheriff was disappointed at not having anyone to arrest.

Psychic Suicide—Solution

(1) Pauline Egremont.   (2) By disguising the time of death with a lens and a remote control.

Once the sergeant figured out the reason the remote control was missing, he knew the killer must be Pauline Egremont, the last person seen in the victim's room. Like Noah and several others, she was being blackmailed by the diabolic psychic. Unlike the others, she had reached her breaking point.

Pauline made the wind chime and hung it in the tree. She also phoned Noah to postpone his session. She needed this hour to make the crime look like suicide.

During her time with the invalid swami, Pauline made him tea and slipped in the poison. As he was dying, she went to work destroying his blackmail files with acid. She then placed the teacup and incense candle near the sunny window. She filled the kettle, set it to boil on the hot plate, then grabbed the remote control and exited, pulling the door locked behind her.

After leaving the house, Pauline sneaked around to the yard and waited until shortly before Noah's arrival. Operating the remote control through the window, she turned on the television and did a little channel surfing. She then removed the central crystal from the wind chime. A double-convex lens focuses light, and like a remote control it works through glass. With this lens, she focused the sun's rays, lighting the incense candle, and keeping the cup of poison nice and hot. The burn on Fred's hand occurred when her aim faltered.

A few minutes later, when the landlady opened the swami's door, she found all the evidence anyone would need to deduce that there had been a fresh suicide. Well, everything except a remote control.

Shot in the Cul-de-Sac — Solution

(1) His neighbor and lover, Wendy Peterson. (2) A crime of passion. (3) Wendy used her official position to tamper with evidence.

Once we assume that someone is trying to frame Marlene Smucker, the question becomes "Who?" Who was alone with the evidence, "carelessly" obliterating some of it? Who performed the autopsy that came up with that incriminating bullet? Wendy Peterson, assistant medical examiner, the same Ms. Peterson who, along with her bothersome dog, lived next door to the Smuckers.

Wendy and Ed were having a neighborly affair while Marlene was off at work. After their final tryst, Ed announced it was over. Wendy seemed to take it well. But later, while Ed was alone with his coffee, Wendy returned with her gun. Her first shot went wide and hit the doorjamb. Her second was right on target.

It was a crime of passion and Wendy fled back home through the bushes. After calming down, she knew she had to return to clean up. In her role as assistant ME, Wendy conned the rookie into leaving her alone. In those few minutes, she retrieved Marlene's gun from the bedroom, expunged her various fingerprints, and "accidentally" replaced her old footprints with new ones, thereby compromising a key piece of evidence.

That night in the woods Wendy fired Marlene's .28 into the tree. She buried the gun in an obvious spot by the highway, then left with the bullet. Later, as she performed the autopsy, Wendy palmed the .22 shell from her gun and replaced it with the .28 shell.

When the chief medical examiner discovered that Wendy lived right next door and didn't own a radio capable of monitoring police bands, the investigation began to focus on her.

The Show Girl Murders—Solution
(1) Dora, accidentally during a fight.   (2) Dora, in order to protect her alibi.   (3) To get rid of the evidence that could wreck her alibi.

The doorman was right about the motive; he just had the casting wrong. Dora, not Deedee, was the other show girl in the love triangle. That afternoon in the dressing room, Dolly confronted her rival. The women fought. The conflict came to an abrupt end when Dora shoved Dolly into the mirror and the glass sliced into her neck. When Tim knocked on the door, Dora had to think fast. She was in costume and her long gloves were torn and bloody. She quickly removed them, taking Dolly's pair from the closet as she ran out the side door.

Dora didn't expect to have an alibi and was surprised when the detective told her she'd been seen with Deedee in the hall. The explanation was obvious. The young man, unfamiliar with the theater, had seen Deedee standing by the mirror and assumed he was seeing two show girls, not one. But this presented a problem. Soon enough, Deedee would be questioned and reveal the truth. Deedee had to die.

The business with the mirror was a desperate move. By breaking it and having it removed, Dora hoped to avoid discovery of how Tim had been fooled. Unfortunately for her, this act simply drew attention to the mirror. After Tim's second interview, the police led him to the side hall, where he realized the truth.

Swallowing the Gun—Solution

(1) Hank told him; the embezzler was Hank's lunch date.
(2) Dr. Hubert Russell.   (3) Russell examined Hank's sore
throat. "Say aah!"

The police focused their investigation on Dr. Hubert Russell,
a general internist. They discovered the doctor's gambling ad-
diction and a 6-month-old bank account with a single large
deposit that had been eaten away by many small withdrawals.
When asked about the deposit, Russell said that he had a tri-
fecta win at the racetrack. Under intense questioning, he broke
down, confirming what the lieutenant already suspected.

"Okay, okay," the doctor confessed. "I dropped by Hank's
office a few minutes before 1:00. We had a lunch date. He was
at his desk looking over some corporation papers. I recognized
them at once. Last year's escrow records—right before we
changed banks. That's when I fiddled with the books, while we
were changing banks. I was going to pay it back. My luck was
just about to change. I could feel it. Anyway, Hank told me
about Barlow's theory. He didn't believe it for a second, good
old Hank. But those papers in his hands were all Barlow would
need to start tracing it back to me.

"We kept chatting. All the time I was desperately trying to
think of some way to get hold of those papers. Anything I did
was just going to arouse his suspicions. And then he started
coughing. All of a sudden Hank had gotten a sore throat. He
figured he was coming down with a cold and asked me to take
a look. People are always asking for free advice."

Russell smiled. "A doctor tells you to open your mouth and
you don't think twice. Then, when he's an inch from your face,
he asks you to lean back and open wider . . . About ten out of
ten close their eyes and say 'Aah!' until you tell them to stop.
Hank's gun was hanging in his holster, a foot away. The temp-
tation was irresistible. Eating the gun, you know, a typical cop
suicide. Then he could take the blame for the money. It seemed
foolproof. What made you suspect?"

Video Violence—Solution

(1) Renaldo wounded himself to gain an alibi, then bled to death.   (2) Renaldo.   (3) Jane played the first killer as a publicity stunt; Renaldo played the second for real.

The confusing bits of evidence begin to make sense when Renaldo is included as a suspect. The television host certainly had reason to kill his wife. Jane was in love with another man (her physical therapist, if you must know) and was planning to divorce Renaldo. As the show's executive producer, she could take him to the cleaners in a divorce.

Renaldo's ratings triumph was based on fraud. The mob didn't feel endangered by "Exposé." Renaldo and Jane had arranged the threatening letters and phone calls. When ratings began to dip, Renaldo came up with a publicity stunt, an attempt on his life caught on video by his own camera operator.

Jane played the role of assassin, appearing in the woods and using blanks. The shot was supposed to miss him completely. So imagine Jane's surprise when Renaldo grasped his leg and "blood" began oozing from it. Jane ran back home, thoroughly confused, leaving the gun and the costume at the prearranged drop, the potting shed.

After purposely sending Gregory in the wrong direction, Renaldo got up and ran to the shed, donning the costume, gloves, mask, and gun. Using the security code, he entered the house, killed his wife, then waited until Fred appeared on the stairs as a witness.

Renaldo discarded the costume in the shed. Returning to the woods, he threw away the extra shell, then came face-to-face with the hardest part, shooting himself. He was planning just to give himself a flesh wound. But he misfired, cutting an artery. Still true to his plan, Renaldo wiped the gun clean and threw it away.

The murderous host tried to tie a tourniquet around his leg, but it was too late. He was already losing consciousness, leaving behind a sensational mystery, not to mention a hit made-for-television movie, produced by Fred and directed by Gregory.

Index